Albion College
Development Office

D0560824

RECEIVED
JUN 3 0 1997
By_____

Raising Big Bucks

The complete guide to producing pledge-based special events

Cindy R. Kaitcer

Bonus Books, Inc., Chicago

© 1996 by Bonus Books, Inc.
All rights reserved

Except for appropriate use in critical reviews or works of scholarship, the repro-
duction or use of this work in any form or by any electronic, mechanical or other
means now known or hereafter invented, including photocopying and recording,
and in any information storage and retrieval system is forbidden without the
written permission of the publisher.

00 99 98 97 96   5 4 3 2 1

Library of Congress Cataloging-in-Publication Data

Kaitcer, Cindy R.
   Raising big bucks : the complete guide to producing pledge-based special
events / Cindy R. Kaitcer.
     p.   cm.
   Includes bibliographical references.
   ISBN 1-56625-059-5
   1. Fund raising—United States—Management.   2. Walk-a-thons—
Management. I. Title.
   HV41.9.U5K35   1996
   658.15′224—dc20   96-27805

Bonus Books, Inc.
160 East Illinois Street
Chicago, Illinois 60611

Printed in the United States of America

In memory of my Grandmother Bea.
Her love, wisdom and strength continue to guide and inspire me.

Table of Contents

Acknowledgments

So many people have helped with the creation of this book, I hardly know where to begin. First of all, I owe a tremendous debt of gratitude to Eve Brouwer of the National Safety Council, my good friend and "agent," for creating the opportunity for me to write this book.

For their friendship and many contributions to this book, I would especially like to thank the following colleagues and friends: Fred Meyer of Ideas To Go, Inc., Kathleen Durkin of the Crohn's and Colitis Foundation of America, Laura Jozaitis, Janet Treuhaft of The Touch of Treuhaft, Diana Naccarato of La Rabida Children's Hospital, Glen Ryniewski of the City of Chicago's Mayor's Office of Special Events, Nancy Roberts Linder of Nancy Roberts Linder Consulting, Kim Glasman of Country Thunder USA, Caroline Cogtella of the City of Chicago, Celeste Watts of Risk Management and Information Systems, Inc., Max Bar-Nahum of The Orensof Groupe and my sister Amy Wise with the March of Dimes. And a special thank you to my friend Randall (Randy) Cronk, MBA and CPA, who contributed greatly to Chapter 4, Budget and Computer Systems.

I would like to single out Tina Garbin of the Colorado Coalition for the Homeless for her contribution of Chapter 3,

Planning: One Step Toward Success. Tina's extraordinary organizational and strategic planning ability make her uniquely qualified to write on planning and its critical components. I value our friendship and appreciate her dedication and commitment to this project.

My sincerest thanks to my dearest friends and family for their continued love, encouragement and understanding while working on this book (and always) — I am truly blessed. In particular, I would like to thank Dr. Joan Leska, Karin Lukas, Beth Solomon, Benita Shobe, Nina Weil, Linda Gasiorowski, Leslie and Mona Kaitcer and my mother and stepfather, Arlene and Jack Hochwarter. A very special thank you to my dear friend Dr. Noam Alperin, who encouraged me daily and never let me give up.

Introduction

Today more and more nonprofit organizations are competing for the diminishing charitable dollar. Pledge-based special events are a fund-raising option that you may choose to add to your development calendar in an attempt to tap into a new donor market. Special events are overrated and underrated. Overrated because they don't suddenly raise a year's operating budget overnight. Underrated because they do much more than raise money . . . they raise community visibility and involvement. Choosing the right event is just the beginning and hard work isn't enough. Planning is critical.

Participatory sporting events are the most exhilarating and engaging events to produce. They have all the elements of a good mystery . . . intrigue, large amounts of money, complex logistical challenges — even danger. As a development professional, you probably know there is no feeling in the world like the end of an event . . . when the dinner auction is over and you sit down and take your shoes off for the first time that day. Or the direct-mail campaign that just yielded revenue 14% over its goal — that's satisfaction. But nothing compares to the first and last participant crossing a finish line in a sporting event. And nothing can compare to the feeling when a physically challenged participant crosses the line. One year, while managing a two-day, 150-mile bike tour, an auburn-haired young woman (around 30) fell off her bicycle on a rural farm road. She had cuts and scrapes on her legs, face and arms and was rushed to a nearby hospital. Though bruised, she demanded to continue (though closely monitored) . . . she had only five miles left to go and she was determined to cross the finish line *unassisted.* As this feisty, bruised and determined woman crossed the line, many spectators wept — not even knowing her carefully guarded secret. She hugged me tightly and whispered, "Thank you. Please don't tell anyone, but I want you to know how much I appreciate the opportunity to have done this event. I have multiple sclerosis — I have been training for this ride for a year and I did it!" We shared a special moment together, struck with the enormity of what she had accomplished — raising thousands for the cause and completing an amazing personal challenge.

I'm certainly not purely altruistic; I don't do events for the warm feeling I get inside and I would venture to say you do not, either. Don't think a development person alive is — we're business people, too. If we're not, we should be! (I'll address this issue in a minute.) This particular moment changed my way of thinking — and my perspective on things. We've all had reasons for doing the repertoire of events we do. But sporting events can heighten or bring back that long-lost feeling for why you got into fund raising in the first place — and bring back some of that idealism that, perhaps, we lost along the way and some we never had. There will be a renewed commitment. I use the word "we," for, as you know, it is a team effort. Development professionals are people who have the talent to cultivate, manage and motivate staff, volunteers and vendors. Goals can only be met, maintained and exceeded by team efforts that rely on the involvement and support of everyone . . . from the CEO or executive director to the members of the board and the volunteers. I read a "letter to the editor" recently in which Brydon M. DeWitt of DeWitt & Associates said "development officers offer individuals the opportunity to invest human energy and talent . . . Successful development officers help others achieve their goals and, in so doing, meet the objectives of their institutions." Kevin Burns, a colleague and currently the Midwestern regional manager for the U.S. Olympic Committee (a nonprofit organization), stated "we are not fund raisers . . . we are **fund-raising managers** . . . we manage the process." I wholeheartedly agree.

Back to the business of business. The most important thing one can learn from this book is to run your event — regardless of your level within the organization — like a **business.** I recently read an article in the financing business section of *Crain's Chicago Business,* titled: "To do good, non-profits now must do well." Jonathan Engman, director of the Chicago Architectural Foundation, stated, "Non-profits are basically small businesses. Like small businesses, they cannot operate without at least the promise of profit: **No margins, no mission.**"

"I truly believe this is the distinctly corporate ethos that all nonprofits need to adopt to survive. And, in the next few years, our sector will have more pressure," stated Thom Clark, director of the Community Media Workshop, a Chicago-based media consulting group. He calls this period of time Darwinian . . . survival-of-the-fittest time. Last year alone, national charitable giving to universities, hospitals, environmental groups and, in particular, international organizations increased between 8% and 20%, depending on the sector, according to the *Chronicle of Philanthropy,* which tracks charitable giving. Donald Haider, director of the Public and Non-Profit Management Program at the J.L. Kellog Graduate School of Management at Northwestern University believes that "Good causes don't guarantee success — they've got to be managed."

Again, I couldn't agree more. Rule #1: An event *must* be managed like a business. You'll notice I never use the walk-a-thon or bike-a-thon in this book (or ever). Quite frankly, I believe the phrase "walk-a-thon" has a "mom and pop" connotation. We should eliminate phrases that connote a mom-and-pop feeling. We need to re-formulate our way of thinking about ourselves, our events and our perceptions. Often, we "undersell" our events — we do not think our events are worthy of big sponsorship dollars. Yes, some times they are not, but **our perceptions and the events must change.** We must start looking at our events as individual profit centers. Each event is like its own business. We need to analyze each event through a battery of analyses.

---

* "To do good, non-profits now must do well," Amy O'Connor, *Crain's Chicago Business,* December 11, 1995.

To illustrate this point, look at the following example: About a year ago I did some consulting for a walk in a large U.S. market. This cause-related walk raised one million dollars with 25,000 participants (let's call this event #1). At first glance, this appears to be a phenomenal feat. In reality, however, it's not. True, it is remarkable getting 25,000 people to the same place at the same time. But with a more careful (and quantitative) examination and by comparing it to other similar events in the market, this is a very poor performance. *How can raising one million dollars be a poor performance?* Well, another walk in the same market and in the same year raised one million dollars — with only 9,000 participants (let's call this event #2). What does this tell us about event #1? Well, it shows us that event #1 had a lower pledge **average** per participant. Event #1's average pledge = $40.00 per participant. Event #2's average pledge = $111.00 per participant. Event #2 not only raised 64% *more* per participant than event #1, but it cost less per participant to produce the event . . . less mailing costs, fewer port-a-potties, less food. In addition, the cost *per capita* is much higher in #2 than in #1. Why such a discrepancy? Event #2 raised more money per person living in its market than event #1. How can event #1 increase its pledge per participant? We will answer this question in Chapter 13, Pledge Collection.

Rule #2: Past success does not guarantee future success. The paradigm shift is the key to any campaign development and analysis. One of the big '90s buzz phrases of corporate America (and in any MBA program) is "paradigm shift." A **paradigm** is a world view that serves as a model or pattern, a prototype. A paradigm shift could be described as "breaking the mold" or "out-of-the-box" thinking. A paradigm shift is a shift away from your old patterns. We must always be aware of the ever-changing "fancy" of the public. Break the mold!

A few years ago, Sears hired a new guy to head up their merchandising group. For years, Sears had poor performance, largely due to their old ways of thinking. Their lack of vision or ability to see things outside of their own paradigm cost them their coveted market share. Sears always saw J.C. Penney and Kmart as their competition — and because Sears was doing better than the two, they thought the status quo was just fine. But they had blinders on and did not see Wal-Mart right behind them . . . and then right in front . . . Wal-Mart came into the discount market and blew Sears away. Why? Because Sears assumed their past success would give them future success. Their thinking was stale. They only saw things from their own viewpoint — retailing. Sears realized what was wrong — they badly needed a strategic thinker from outside their business to see clearly. They brought in the former president of A.C. Nielson, a market research guy. Sears' profits soared. The "guy," John Costello, had the ability to think strategically and knew almost nothing about retailing. His vision had no blinders from the past and this has contributed greatly to Sears' newfound success in the marketplace. Because of Sears' myopic thinking, they — temporarily — gave up their claim as one of America's success stories. What does the Sears loss of market share have to do with the design of a campaign? *Everything.*

I learned the hard way; perhaps you have, too. It isn't fun and it isn't pretty. As development professionals, we are generally a controlling bunch of folks. Sorry, but we probably wouldn't be successful in our field if we weren't a little controlling (and a bit crazy)! As a group we tend to be myopic. I believe we *think* we are looking at a problem or challenge with new insight, but, most often, it's not possible to change our way of thinking without getting input from others outside our own vantage point. Similar to creating a name in Chapter 5, we must bring others in from all areas within our organization and, especially, from outside our organization. And from all levels. One can never underestimate the contributions an entry-level staff member can make . . . or an event participant who raised a mere $22.00. Because they see our world from a new and different view, they can often give us insights we never would have, or could have, arrived at.

So, again, you're asking, why is this important to us in the nonprofit world? Well, it is important to learn this lesson — preferably by studying it, not experiencing it — now, rather than later when an event fails. If one can grasp this concept, ideas can be limitless — and have a great impact on everything from participant recruitment to event evaluation. I have, at times, been able to train myself to think this way, asking others to be a part of the process. Sometimes, though, my past reality gets in the way of truly creative new ideas. Often it's best to give others a strategic task and ask them to bring their findings to you. This way, like Sears, you will not bring your old vision of how something *should* be done.

For example, when you want some new suggestions for incentives to participate (prizes), ask a couple of past prize-winners. I strongly recommend this concept! Incorporate this type of **paradigm shift** into your campaign development process.

If you've tried pledge-based events before and have been disappointed with results . . . read on. *This book is a comprehensive guide — a formula for success.*

At the risk of sounding dramatic, producing a sporting event, especially a multiple-site walking event, will be one of the most difficult challenges you will ever face in fund raising — and perhaps your life. It will take a lot of time, energy and persistence, but the rewards, especially financial, *will* be there. Guaranteed.

While this book focuses on a pledge-based walk, nearly every principle outlined can be tailored to any other event (especially bike tours and runs) —even donor-based campaigns. Some of you might be planning your first walk and some are walk veterans; I've tried to include information for a broad-based reference. Regardless, please keep in mind that the examples in this book are just that . . . examples. You must continually tailor these principles and strategies to fit the needs of your own market, community, organization, etc.

Dollars are important; after all, nonprofits are money-driven organizations, but never, never compromise your cause or mission. I urge you to stay focused on what's really important. Or, as my late father used to say, "Keep your eye on the donut, not the hole."

One

Why a
Pledge-Based Event?

Profit Potential

We all know the variety of fund-raising events out there, but few have the profit potential of pledge-based events. Walks in particular can have *substantial growth* as well as inherent benefits, such as building a base of future contributors and corporate matching/sponsorship prospects, which will be discussed shortly.

While managing the Super Cities Walk for Multiple Sclerosis™, Chicago Chapter, we experienced phenomenal growth, increasing revenue by 895% (from $114,000 to $1,002,000) and participants by 695% (from 1,200 to nearly 10,000) in less than four years — and you can, too. Perhaps your market does not have the same dollar potential as Chicago (the third-largest market in the country), but your results in terms of *percentages* can be similar — or even better.

In a country where nearly half of all health clubs offer some type of walking program, and where walking shoe sales are a 185 billion dollar business (not to mention the fastest-growing seg-

1

ment of the athletic shoe industry)*, it's easy to see why pledge-based walks are an attractive market for any nonprofit. "Walking is the number one form of exercise in the U.S. — more than 70 million Americans walk for fitness," says Dr. Daniel Kirschenbaum, professor and director of Northwestern University Medical School. A leading sports psychologist, prophetic author and researcher, Dr. Kirschenbaum is a consultant to professional athletic organizations, including national basketball players and the United States Olympic Committee. In addition, 62% of all kids walk and 58% bike for exercise**, which makes a walking event a perfect family outing.

Dr. Kirschenbaum recommends walking for a number of reasons, including to increase one's metabolic rate, ease the symptoms of stress, decrease depression, improve digestion and build strength. Additionally, 95% of people who have successfully lost weight *maintain their weight loss exercise almost every day.* Regardless of actual weight loss, most women try to lose weight every year and *want to exercise,* Dr. Kirschenbaum reiterated. Some very solid reasons to target these individuals for an event.

In addition, almost anyone can walk, so the market potential is greater than nearly any other event. As you well know, the target market for a dinner campaign, auction or even golf outing is much more narrowly defined as many cannot afford the often pricey entrance fee or ticket. Further, after a dinner campaign is said and done, the organization is often left with 100 to 1,000 attendees who — with the exception of the few benefactors or event sponsors — will give their ticket price, perhaps bid on an auction item, and they're off . . . sometimes never to be seen again. I'm certainly not knocking dinners and other donor-based campaigns — as you know, dinners are wonderful to attract new board members, build a base of future corporate donors and can be phenomenal revenue producers and image enhancers, but often with high expense ratios, as the dinner portion is always a direct benefit to the donor and is rarely, if ever, sponsored. A walk or bicycle tour can be a wonderful complement to any not-for-profit

---

* Urban Trekker, *Bazaar,* Elizabeth O'Brien, September 1995.
** "Kids and Exercise," *Healthy, Wealthy & Wise,* August 1995.

organization, especially ones which may have a tendency to be "top heavy" in the "same ol'" campaigns. It is especially critical in the recruitment of future volunteers, including board members. Since most people can walk, walking events attract people from all socioeconomic and educational levels. And don't forget about that "out-of-the-box" thinking — create your own niche pledge-based event, such as a motorcycle ride or pet walk.

That market potential is there. But you're probably asking yourself, "Hey self, is she crazy? What about all that competition in sporting events, especially walks? Every charity is getting on the band wagon!" It's true. A lot of organizations have gotten in-volved, but many do not know how to market it and make their cause *compelling,* invite participants back — and, most important, collect pledges! Frankly, many do not understand how complex logistics really are. Often we are great at recruiting participants but get in too deep, and after one bad year of not delivering what you've promised, you're out of the game. You'll not only lose pledges, but also future participants — and future donors. I'm certainly not suggesting that if you skim this book you'll be an expert. It will take a lot of hard work, research and planning. Regardless, the market is there and will be there. As Dr. Kirsch-enbaum states above, more than 100 million people walk for exer-cise — that's nearly 50% of *your* community. They're out there, just waiting for you to lure them to your event.

Building a Base for Direct Mail and Corporate Matching Programs

An almost always overlooked byproduct of a successful walk is not only the participants who participate in your event, but their sponsors (people who make pledges to them). Perhaps obvi-ous to you, I discovered this quite accidentally! In fact, I was long into a walk campaign in 1990 when I noticed a donor pledged $500 to a participant. Wanting to acknowledge his kind gift to the campaign, I sent off a quick thank you — and it stopped there. The following year, after a bike tour ended and as pledges were just beginning to come in, I noticed that the pledge sheets of the bike tours had significantly higher pledges than ever before. As I looked through the mounds of pledge sheets (complete with each donor's name, address and amount of pledge), I saw yet another large pledge. As you know, it's rare to see more than a $50 pledge from any individual sponsor of a friend, relative or co-worker, let alone a $250 one. From that day forward, I scoured the returned pledge forms, adding donors of more than $100 to our existing mailing list. After all, people who donate more than $100 to an individual walker or bike tour participant must have some connection to the cause — and we sent them literature on the event, future events, and our chapter newsletter. As our participant base grew, we were no longer able to do this by hand, and a computer code was born to assign to each $100+ donor. First, acknowledgments were sent, thanking these people for their contributions and congratulating them on their help in making a difference. Then there were those companies who sponsored an individual. . . . we hit them up, too. We asked some to consider setting up a corporate team — all of these we added to our chapter mailing list.

On the corporate side, we also identified individuals who sent in corporate matching funds (or matching gifts as some organizations call it). Corporate matching gifts, as you know, are one of the fastest and easiest ways in which to double — even triple — pledge dollars. And corporations who have established corporate matching programs make the best targets for corporate teams. We'll talk more about the recruitment of corporate teams in Chapter 11, Catching Your Target Market's Eye.

As you can see, a pledge-based event can significantly impact your organization — in increased revenue, awareness and image enhancement.

Two

Anatomy of a Pledge

We all know the definition of a pledge — unfortunately, too often it is something that is made, but not turned in. It is safe to say that the most important part of a pledge-based event is the pledge and its collection. While not desirable, marketing, public relations, sponsorships and even logistics can be a bit off and the event will probably be a success if people show up. But if the pledges aren't paid — no matter how aesthetically pleasing the walk path was — the event will be a failure. This is not to say these components aren't integral parts of an event. But if one or even two break down, you can still have a financially successful event. I've had the good fortune (with the help of great volunteers) to pull off a financially successful event when a storm occurred and the turnout was at only 55%. Normal turnout for walks works out to be 100% — 20% of registered walkers typically don't show, but 20% walk on. A pre-prepared letter went out the day after the event to all the "no-shows" asking them to ride on their own and still collect the pledges. It worked, and 38% of the no-shows sent in their pledges. It's all in components of the pledge and its collection. Pledge collection will be discussed at greater length in Chapter 13.

Pricing the Campaign

Back to the anatomy of a pledge. The most important component is pricing the campaign. For example, what is the minimum required to receive a t-shirt? Should we charge a fee? Should we have a pledge minimum? The first rule is never underestimate the value of your event. It may seem like all you're giving them for a walk, for instance, is three to five hours of physical labor and blisters. I've made this mistake too many times. After event evaluations come back (and participants come back the next year), one gets the message that there is more than altruism at work here. People do events for different reasons. I met one of my dearest friends through a walking event. He signed on as a volunteer to meet women. My friend Nina and her family walk every year — not only because a family friend has MS, but it's a great family outing. There is relatively nothing one can do for under 10 or 15 bucks these days, let alone a family of four. Further, as we all know, participants rarely — if ever — pay their pledge out of their own pockets. The majority collect pledges from family, friends, neighbors and co-workers. And most do it for the incentives and other intrinsic benefits such as exercise, meeting friends and being with co-workers in an "out of the office" setting. Back in 1991 I conducted a survey of 10% of 10,000 participants (1,000) who had just completed a walk (we caught them shortly after crossing the finish line, before having lunch). More than 87% of the people surveyed said they participated because it was helping someone with a devastating disease. Yet, when given the option on their prize forms to donate their prize back to the charity (they were allowed to keep the ever-popular t-shirt), less than 3% elected to do so. *So much for altruism!*

I was a firm believer in "if they show up, give 'em a t-shirt." That was one year with pathetically sluggish "sales" (pledges). I moved on to "if they pledge $25, give 'em a t-shirt." Pledges inched slightly higher, but still many people showed up, ate our food, drank our water, got a t-shirt and had a great time, but *never paid a dollar of their pledge.* Which brought me to a new and highly recommended philosophy — run the walk like a *business,* from the budget to pledge collection. Price competitively. Don't give anything away free except food or items that have been sponsored or donated. I strongly recommend that any pledge-based campaign (sporting event or not) have *a minimum pledge amount as a policy.* NO exceptions. It may be hard for you and/or committee members to swallow, but you'll appreciate the tip later. *This is not to say that participants must pay their pledge the day of the event.* It is *preferable* and you should definitely consider creating incentives to encourage day-of payments (perhaps by giving t-shirts on event day only to individuals who pay at least the minimum pledge . . . or create a new club for people who pay more than $100.00 on event day). I'm not talking about a *fee* per se (although fees are particularly necessary for bicycle tours, which have much higher per-registrant costs due to t-shirts, bib numbers and more mailings per participant). However, I do believe a realistic price should be determined. This helps in more ways than one . . . it takes not-for-profit events out of the "mom-and-pop" arena and puts them in line with other entertainment venues. Something crucial for survival. As you know, there are still a lot of mom-and-pop events out there all fighting the budget battle. However, you mustn't succumb to the "We don't have the budget so we can't do it" tales of woe. If you approach pricing your campaign like a business, you'll never be without "bells and whistles" again! Here's how to price a campaign:

- Work backwards. Do a complete, intensive budget first (see Chapter 4) before passing "go."
- Search in your own backyard. Look at any past pledge-based events. Call other charities and ask what their average pledge is.
- Research similar "for profit" activities (ice-skating, bowling, video arcades, movies [include the price of concessions!], etc.) Don't forget to add value-added items like food — lunch and/or rest-stop items, give-aways from sponsors or coupons to the "cost" of your event. And never, never underestimate the value of your event. But never charge a registration fee.
- Don't forget that people rarely pay pledges out of their own pocket. If you've created good incentives (prizes) for participants, you'll have no problem.

Now, having said all the above, *don't get too out of control.* We must be careful not to *overprice!*

Here's a sampling of what the campaign standards are in terms of pledges for some charity walks:

Charity	Min. Pledge to participate	Min. for prizes	Fee
March of Dimes *Walk America*	$25 minimum	$75 for t-shirt	no
The Aids Walk	No minimum, but a $150 goal is suggested	$100 for t-shirt	no
MS *Super Cities Walk* (note: $35 registration fee for 2 day bicycle tour)	Recommended $50	$100	no
American Diabetes	$50, but no one turned away	includes t-shirt	no
La Rabida *Walk for Kids*	$25	$25	no

You and I know that these are average, generalized standards. They must not be used without doing the homework. The homework is the often-exhausting "B" word (budget). Once the budget is determined for *your specific and unique market,* you can proceed in pricing.

If you remember one thing, always have a *suggested minimum dollar amount for participation. Remember, participants are rarely taking the money out of their own pockets!*

Determining the Minimum Pledge

After deciding how to price the campaign, it is important to shift your focus to setting goals per participant. Overall campaign goals cannot be reached without this important element. For a walk campaign, my experience shows that a goal of $100 per participant is a good place to start. A detailed, itemized budget must be completed before continuing. Special circumstances in your market may impact greatly. Obviously, if unemployment is at 22% in your market, a $100 minimum pledge for a walk would be considered an unrealistic goal. But if the average household income is greater than $75,000 (e.g., Greenwich, Connecticut), then this amount would be too low. If the cost to the organization is $36 per participant, then the minimum pledge must obviously include the cost plus the total amount to be raised per person — plus a cushion for the unexpected (low turn-out, pledge collection, etc.). While obvious to most veteran fund-raising professionals, these variables are some of the most overlooked and avoided areas — and the largest opportunity to *not* raise money.

As stated earlier, any data from *any* other past pledge-based campaign is the best place to begin. Ask yourself what was the average pledge? What did the participants receive (food, snacks, coupons, a good time)? Research your community's employment rate, average household income, etc. Most of this information is easily accessible through any department of economic development or planning/zoning department. If your market does not have a planning department, check with the local chamber of commerce, an often forgotten and invaluable resource.

Once the minimum pledge is set, there are a number of ways to increase per-participant revenue. However, these mostly have to do with pledge collection and incentives, not in pricing the campaign. More on this in Chapter 6 (Communications Development), Chapter 10 (Incentives to Participate) and Chapter 13 (Pledge Collection).

Three

Planning: One Step Toward Success

A walk or any special event is an overwhelming job. It is time consuming and energy consuming. It is expensive. The only way to maximize profits and minimize headaches is through well-constructed planning. This process takes something huge and breaks it down into achievable tasks. One of the most difficult challenges facing special event fund raisers is the ability to think big, while thinking small, through all the details. Once you are underway with organizing an event, unless everything is well thought out, even the most obvious details can be easily overlooked. *Planning is critical.*

This chapter outlines the components of a strategic marketing plan and provides a sample timeline that demonstrates the breadth of details necessary for execution. Allow plenty of time for planning. A year in advance isn't too soon to start on major events.

Consider the following tips for the planning stage:

- Turn your most successful fund raiser into a major annual event to avoid competing with yourself.

- Keep detailed records for next year; the best events evolve over time.
- Make the most of community resources. Don't be afraid to ask for support — students, businesses, employee groups, civic organizations, churches. Ask them to be sponsors, participants, underwriters.
- Volunteers are the cornerstone of every event. Nonprofits are not only competing for dollars, but for volunteer time and talents. Thank and recognize volunteers even for the smallest tasks. Treat them with respect and explain their role in "the big picture." If they know that you genuinely appreciate them, you will win their allegiance.
- Consider putting together a committee of volunteers and staff to brainstorm all conceivable details to ensure that all bases are covered. Often the key staff person is "too close" to the event to recognize a missing piece.
- No amount of planning can make up for poor organization. You must be able to put it all together for success. If current staff lack organizational skills and are not detail oriented, rethink your assignments.
- Develop a planning schedule and stick to it. Plan your work and work your plan.
- Be prepared for the worst. As soon as everything is running like clockwork, the sky will open and lightning will strike. This is a business where the only thing you can't plan for is the one thing that can change all plans.

A Word About Repeat Events: Evaluate

If this is a repeat event, prior to the planning process, it is necessary to have a complete and thorough evaluation of the previous year's campaign. In order to conduct an evaluation you should:

A. Tabulate participant evaluation responses. Type up all negative comments so they can be addressed.

B. Gather the following statistical information for as many years as your records allow:

- Total number of registrants, participants and no-shows
- Total amount pledged
- Total amount paid
- Collection average

C. Gather any demographic, psychographic, geographic and behavioral information from previous surveys to better define your target market. If event evaluations do not include this information, revise them.

D. Compare budgeted expenses to actual dollars spent in each budgetary category. Determine cause of over-runs or shortfalls.

E. Prepare a final tracking summary of all past participants to identify the best sources of participants, past participants, street distribution, direct mailing, etc.

Once all of this information is gathered, set aside some time to review the results will all fund-raising staff. Critical questions that should be answered at the end of this evaluation include:

- Are there additional areas into which we should expand the event?
- How effectively did we utilize and acknowledge corporate sponsors?
- Did we create a full menu of recruitment strategies? What new strategies can we introduce next year? What strategies are no longer effective?
- Learn from your mistakes and successes. Evaluate every aspect of your event. If an event takes up too much time and raises too little money, think twice about it next year.

Should You Have a Multi-Activity Event?

The best way to make a walking event more fun, festive and confusing — and raise more money — is to incorporate one or two more different events into the existing event. Obviously, the more types of events, the greater variety and number of people you can attract.

What types of events work well with a walk?

1) **Rollerblading** (as long as there is sufficient room on both sides of walkers).

2) **Wheelchair** (again, as long as there are provisions for accessibility).

3) **Running.** Most walks do not incorporate this into their event, but I don't think it hurts as long as it is made clear it is a non-timed walk! Runners usually live and die by the clock. Furthermore, runners are a lot more aggressive and may knock into people if your path is not wide enough. And runners are significantly faster than walkers (average mile = 9 minutes vs. 20 minutes per walker). Therefore, your rest stops need to be opened a lot earlier (unless you have runners start later). And runners, by the way, generally don't make great fund raisers.

4) **Stroller Brigade.** This is fun and encourages people to bring out additional fund raisers . . . however, don't expect that kid in the stroller to raise money — it's great if his/her parent raises money for the kid, but don't be too rigid about minimum pledges for the little tykes! Also, strollers can be annoying to walkers. Last caution: People pushing strollers tend to be much slower and also cannot go the full distance. Make sure you have plenty of provisions for picking these people up should they need transportation back to the start.

Key Components of the Strategic Marketing Plan

The first step in planning is a well thought out strategic marketing plan. "Marketing? But we're just trying to raise money for a good cause." True. Your event will sell itself to those with a vested interest in your mission. To some, no sales pitch is needed and your work is done. Unfortunately, it is not time to go home yet. Most people give money to satisfy their own needs rather than to satisfy the needs of a worthy cause. The majority of your participants, over 90% in most cases, must be *sold.* This puts a different face on your nice, friendly charity event and introduces vocabulary into your plan such as "unique selling proposition" and "target market." The reality is that your event must be thought of as a *product,* plain and simple. Your challenge is to build "brand loyalty."

Marketing is the total process by which an organization brings an event to a market. It considers the dynamics of the market, target market, event image, objectives, strategies, tactics, budget and culminates with a timeline. Each component builds on the next and the plan will not be effective if any of its elements are short-changed.

Dynamics of the Market

Time must be set aside during the planning stages to study your market. Determining your competitive advantage may be one of the most important steps you take toward a successful event. If your market already has too many established walks, put a new twist on your walk. Try something that's never been done before. Shift the paradigm! Think out-of-the-box! Competitive information to gather includes event types, dates, locations, fees and anticipated size. Plot them on a large calendar and carefully examine for your opportunity to create a unique niche in the market.

Identifying the Market

As mentioned, walks are best at generating community visibility and new donors. Clarifying the audience of your event in concrete terms will help keep planning goal-oriented. To increase the likelihood of attracting the right donors you must conduct a market analysis to determine the following:

- Who do you want to tap as a potential donor? This includes demographic, psychographic, geographic and behavioral information.
- Determine not only the kinds of activities that will appeal to this group, but the ones that will seem the freshest and most exciting. Is it possible to put a new twist on an old idea?

Not enough stress can be put on the proper and accurate identification of the target audience. For example, stating "all adults" as your target market may sound ambitious, but you will be much more successful at recruiting "all active, outdoor-oriented, upwardly mobile adults, ages 21–35" than you will recruiting "all adults."

If this is a repeat event, your best audience is the one you already have — past participants. We'll talk more about this lucrative market throughout the book. Put them to work. A large percentage of your new registrants (up to 40% in most cases) will sign up for an event because a friend asked them. Give your past participants exclusive information about the event during planning stages, and ask them to start spreading the word (after all, the event will be more enjoyable for them if they are with friends). In your recruitment plan be sure to add perks and bonuses for past participants. They will not only increase your recruitment force, but they tend to raise more money each year they participate.

Event Image

Think *big*. With special events, it takes the same amount of planning time and almost the same amount of effort to make a large profit as it does to make a smaller one. Expand your event as much as possible. Your event's unique selling proposition (USP) must be identified and highlighted. If yours doesn't have one, it must be created and incorporated into the event. USPs can be based on event type, length, level of challenge, prize structure, celebrity spokesperson and/or theme, etc. The bottom line is that your event must stand out among a crowd or the word "crowd" will never be associated with your event.

Determine whether your walk is appropriate to the market you are trying to reach, and if it is appropriate to the image of your organization. Is it cutting edge or traditional? Prestigious or common? Does your walk concept create an aura that will make it "the place to be" for those you wish to attract? See Chapter 5 for ways to make your cause compelling. Other considerations:

- People are busy. Your walk must promise a rewarding use of their time, and it must deliver.
- Determining the "charge" (minimum pledges and minimum for prizes) for the event can be tricky.

Once the target market is defined you must determine the avenues through which you can advertise the chosen event to reach the broadest segment of the desired market.

Marketing Objectives

For the most part, marketing objectives deal in numbers. They are used to quantify event goal and income expectations. For example, one marketing objective would be to recruit 1,000 participants and raise a net income of $250,000. What you state as objectives are frequently the standards by which your event can and should be evaluated.

Marketing Strategies

The marketing strategy is a grand plan. It deals with the complete operation of taking an event to a market and is formulated only after all the homework has been done. So what's the difference between the objective and the strategy? An objective is the goal you're aiming for. A strategy is your method of achieving that goal. For example, a marketing strategy would be to utilize direct mail, advertising and promotions to reach stated marketing objectives.

Tactics

These are the specific steps you are going to take to achieve your objectives. For example, one tactic may be to distribute 200,000 four-color brochures to 10,000 outlets by February 1. You must consider the kinds of publicity most likely to attract those in your target market. Promotions that are unique and visual have a better chance of gaining attention. Frequency is crucial. Advertisers believe it takes three exposures for consumers to retain an idea or product in memory. Ideally you should use as many vehicles as possible to deliver the message to your target market. Answer the who, what, where, when, why and how questions in all print materials. Evaluate the effectiveness of the following media possibilities based on capturing your target market, cost effectiveness, frequency and creative potential:

- Television
- Radio
- Direct Mail
- Newspapers

- Magazines
- Brochure Distribution
- Billboards
- Flyers

Budget

Develop a budget from day one. Be realistic. Pursue a special event only if your projections indicate your desired goals can be reached. This may sound obvious, but too often nonprofits waste valuable time and money by jumping into an event and falling short of their own "pie in the sky" projections. When this occurs, morale is lost right along with profits.

Project both net income and costs in your budget. Net income, not gross, is the bottom line: An event can bring in very large dollars yet fail to bring in a profit because of the costs incurred. The bottom line must be top-of-mind from day one of planning to final pledge collections. This is critical, particularly during current consumer scrutinizations of nonprofits spending decisions. A generally accepted overhead expense for a special event is within 25 to 30 percent of income. Review this sample budget for a walk prior to constructing your budget.

Sample Expense Breakout

Printing and artwork	35%
Awards and prizes	18%*
T-shirts and promotional items	10%*
Food and beverages	2%
Vehicles	4%
Postage and shipping	15%*
Port-a-potties	2%
Street distribution staff	4%
Other (telephone, travel, meetings, temporary clerical staff)	10%
Total	**100%**

*Can be reduced significantly through sponsorships and outsourcing.

Support

The most successful special events result from a team effort. Does your staff have the time and talent to pull it off? Do you have a sufficient volunteer pool willing to be involved? Can this event attract new volunteers? Do you have the board's approval? Support from all aspects within the organization must be solidified before moving forward. If you do not have internal support, you cannot expect people outside of the organization to support it.

At this point, if you have a unique, appealing event designed for a specific target market with clearly stated objectives, strategies and tactics and a realistic budget, the final step is to develop a timeline.

Timeline

The complexities of organizing an event of any size cannot be comprehended until they are put on paper with date, task and responsibility clearly defined. Once all responsibilities have been outlined, work backwards from the event and determine how much time each task will take. A carefully thought out timeline is necessary if you expect all phases of the campaign to come together on time.

Sample Walk Timeline

Date	Task	Responsibility
Year-round	• Identify potential committee members • Cultivate participants through letters, newsletters and phone calls to top fund raisers • Sponsor cultivation through letters, newsletters, phone calls and personal visits	
9 Months Prior	• Conduct a thorough evaluation of previous campaigns	

7 Months Prior	• Select event chairperson • Send out invitations for first committee meeting (follow-up with phone calls) • Choose an event site/route

6 Months	• First committee meeting — Designate leaders for sub-committees:
	  ▪ Route
	  ▪ Logistics
	  ▪ Media
	  ▪ Sponsorship
	  ▪ Recruitment
	• Research and begin soliciting sponsorship
	  ▪ Cash
	  ▪ In-kind
	  ▪ Media

5 Months	• Confirm routes — begin designating alternate routes (e.g., more challenging, easy, etc.) • Meet with all municipalities along your route, confirm roads, access, permit requirements, etc. • Conduct zip code analysis of previous participants and plot out on mass distribution map • Check all mailing lists and purge duplicates • Research prize structure • Begin writing brochure • Committee meeting(s)
4 Months	• First past-participant mailing to announce early registration benefits • Begin to recruit day-of volunteers • Recruit brochure distributors • Mailing to past teams • Finalize all sponsors • Confirm prize structure • Finalize brochure — send to printer • Write and produce all registrant packet pieces • Hire brochure distributors

- Mail special registration form to previous year's top fund raisers announcing incentives
- Design t-shirt
- Begin personal team recruitment
- Committee meeting(s)
- Recruitment/promotion

3 Months
- Begin brochure mass distribution
- Make personal phone calls to previous top fundraisers and teams who have not registered
- Begin media campaign — send press releases to all local media
- Coordinate equipment plan
- Coordinate food plan
- Coordinate safety plan and write safety manual
- Order t-shirts
- Committee meeting(s)
- Recruitment/promotion

2 Months
- Restock brochures at targeted "hot" areas
- Prepare day-of event materials
- Write volunteer handbook
- Order day-of signs (start/finish, sponsor, etc.)
- Committee meeting(s)
- Recruitment/promotion

1 Month
- Order any vehicles not donated
- Mailing to all current registrants with event updates and day-of logistical information
- Prepare evaluations
- Send out day-of volunteer jobs
- Volunteer training
- Final surveying of route
- Finalize logistics
- Committee meeting(s)
- Recruitment/promotion

Day Before Event	• Mark route(s) • Deliver supplies • Final confirmation with all vendors
Day of Event	• Complete invoices to participants and mail
Day After	• Return all vehicles and supplies
Week After Event	• Write and mail all sponsor thank yous • Send no-show mailing • Send follow-up press release to media • Begin to order prizes
4 Weeks After	• Recruit volunteers to compile evaluations • Hold committee de-briefing and evaluation • Collect pledges
6 Weeks After	• Victory party with all participants, volunteers, sponsors • Collect pledges/evaluate status of pledges
7 Weeks After	• Begin telemarketing for pledge chasers and tele-collecting — continue for six weeks
13 Weeks After	• Send final pledge chaser letter/appeal

The time, energy, expense and attention to detail required for a successful event are not fully realized until the day after . . . when the last truck has been returned to the rental office and the leftover food has been dropped off at the food bank. No manual can describe the overwhelming feeling of satisfaction after the completion of an event. When it's all said and done you should have more money in the bank, new donor names in the database and an increased visibility in your community. Plan to enjoy this brief moment because before you know it, it's time to start planning for next year!

Four

Creating a Budget and Computer Systems

The Budget

In simple terms, the campaign budget is a financial plan that organizes the organization's resources over a period of time to produce a profit. The **profit,** or the money you make over what you spent on the event, is used to provide program services, assistance and/or funding for research for the organization and its cause. The profit can also be used as seed money to begin other programs or special events, such as a pledge-based walk.

When I first started out as a special event coordinator many years ago, I must admit I didn't really know what a budget was. I certainly never thought about income and expense ratios. Of course I knew the basics, but I really didn't know how to go about doing a budget. I recall the chaos of not having any procedures in place. For instance, if I needed to order 15 port-a-potties at $50 each for our event, I would simply give my purchase order to our office manager and she would order. That was the end of that. No recording. No tracking. And no realistic cost for the event. Well, the good ol' days of not keeping track have come and gone.

Today, however, nonprofits must be accountable — to their donors, to the public and to the IRS.

A few years ago, I was asked to do my first comprehensive walk/special event budget. Scared, not knowing much about budgeting, I worked hard to produce it. Not having any preconceived ideas of what a budget should include was probably the best thing I had in my corner; I included every little thing I could think of. My naiveté actually helped me in this process. The "model" I created was then refined (using real accounting terms) by our organization's director of finance, Randall Cronk. Over the years, Randy and I revised it numerous times as we tailored it to meet specific needs of other events. I recommend his budget, Exhibit 4.1, for any pledge-based event.

To track the budget, I recommend keeping separate tracking sheets for each account, e.g., one for postage, one for equipment, etc. (see Budget Tracking Form, Exhibit 4.2). Of course, any good spreadsheet program can do the same thing (being a bit of a dinosaur, I prefer to do this by hand!). Do not under any circumstances wait for reports from your accounting department — it is important that *you* know where you are at every moment! As you can see in this example, it is imperative to not only know how much you have to spend overall, but how much you have remaining in the budget as you go along. As you review this exhibit, you can clearly see that this simple way of tracking expenses *cumulatively* forces the event manager to see exactly where he or she is *at any given time.* Fantasy days are over and we must be responsible and accountable.

A great tool to further track expenses and manage the budget is to list an account name (e.g., postage, printing, etc.), its annual budget, as well as the dollars remaining in the budget directly on the bottom of every purchase order. This allows the person who signs off on purchase orders (usually the director of development or executive director) to make an educated decision. It also serves as a glaring red flag. For example, if you are two months into the planning of your walk and have not begun working on logistics, and you only have $487 left in your equipment rental account in your budget, which started out with $2,600, something is obviously wrong. Where did all the budgeted equipment dollars go? Perhaps the culprit is simply an old invoice from the previous year, or perhaps the event coordinator filling out the forms mis-

BUDGET FOR YEAR			TOTAL: $_____ EVENT CODE:_____ STAFF PERSON:_____		WALK BUDGET:_____ DATE:_____	

SOURCES OF INCOME	ACCT #		CURRENT YEAR BUDGET	PREVIOUS YEAR BUDGET	PREVIOUS YEAR ACT. PROJ.	NEXT YEAR FORECAST
ACCOUNT NAME						
REGISTRATIONS						
FEES						
SPONSORSHIPS						
OTHER						
TOTAL INCOME						
EXPENSES						
SALARIES	145	⇐				
MEDICAL						
FICA						
PENSION						
UNEMPLOYMENT TAX						
PRINTING & ARTWORK						
POSTAGE						
UPS						
FEDERAL EXPRESS						
MESSENGER						
PROGRAM SUPPLIES						
DUES AND SUBSCRIPTIONS						
TRAVEL						
MEETINGS						
EQUIPMENT RENTAL						
AWARDS AND PRIZES						
RETURNED CHECKS						
COMMITTEE MEETINGS						
DISBURS. TO INDIVIDUALS						
AWARDS AND PRIZES						
RETURNED CHECKS						
IN-KIND						
TELEPHONE						
OFFICE SUPPLIES						
COMPUTER SUPPLIES						
PROFESSIONAL FEES						
PARKING						
GENERAL MEETING						
STAFF MEETINGS						
RENT						
UTILITIES						
LIABILITY INSURANCE						
OFFICE EQUIPMENT						
AUDIT						
TOTAL EXPENSE						
NET INCOME						

> assign a different number for each accounting "NAME," e.g., salaries is assigned #145

(Exhibit 4.1) A budget is one of the most important elements in planning an event. You may need to tailor your budget after the first year as your needs change. In addition to the elements on this and the following six pages, you'll also need to budget for UPS and Federal Express charges, meetings, prizes, and food and drink.

takenly charged supplies to equipment rental. Regardless, you must always be on top of where you (or your event manager) is in terms of how much you have, where it is going and why, and what the bottom line is.

	ACCT #	INCOME PER UNIT	NUMBER OF UNITS	TOTAL INCOME
INCOME DETAIL WALK **WORKSHEET**			STAFF PERSON:_____	
DESCRIPTION				
1 REGISTRATIONS		$100	2,100	$210,000
2				
3 PRE-REGISTRATIONS		$150 (past participantsnts)	750	$112,500
4				
5				
6				
7				
8 DAY OF REGISTRATIONS		$76	420	$31,920
9				
10				
11				
12				
13				
14				
15 FEES				
16				
17				
18 SPONSORSHIP				$5,650
19				
20				
21				
22				
23				
24				
25 OTHER				
26				
27				
28				
29				
30				
31 IN-KIND				$7,000
32 RADIO				
33 TV				
34				
35				
36				
37				
38				
39				
40				
41				
42				
43				

(Exhibit 4.1 *continued*)

The budget is the single most important planning tool. As I'm certain you have already experienced, you cannot produce a financially successful event without a budget. Creating a budget is tough, but sticking to it and managing it is even tougher. Exhibit 4.1 should help simplify things for your organization when embarking on or refining your pledge-based walk. Please note, however, that this is a comprehensive budget which was

PRINTING AND ARTWORK | BUDGET FOR YEAR

ACCOUNTING NUMBER:

DESCRIPTION	SIZE	OTHER UNIT	PRICE PER UNIT	NUMBER OF UNITS	TOTAL COST
BROCHURES					
LAYOUT					
ARTWORK					
PHOTOGRAPHS					
SPECIAL PAPER FOR PRINTING					
PRINTING					
TRANSCRIPTS					
AWARD CERTIFICATES					
BROCHURES					
CAMERA-READY ARTWORK					

(Exhibit 4.1 *continued*)

designed for high-end, multi-site walks (I consider a high-end walk to include lots of frills — special benefits to donors such as lunch, etc.). Naturally, you will have to tailor this budget to meet the needs of *your* market, budget and type of event. For example, it may not be necessary to serve lunch at your walk or other give-aways. As we discussed, it is critical to carve out your own niche, making your walk unique. If, for example, you decide to have a

POSTAGE | **BUDGET FOR YEAR** [   ]

ACCOUNTING NUMBER: _____

a DESCRIPTION	SIZE b	OTHER UNIT c	PRICE PER UNIT d	NUMBER OF UNITS e	TOTAL COST f
PRE-EVENT NEWSLETTERS &					
BROCHURES TO PAST PARTICIPANTS					
BULK BROCHURES					
REGISTRATION PACKAGES					
EVENT NEWSLETTER #1					
EVENT NEWSLETTER #2					
FOLLOW-UP NEWSLETTER					
DAY OF EVENT CHASER #1					
POSTCARD REPLY					
STAMPS					
GENERAL CORRESPONDENCE					
ADDRESS CORRECTION					

AVERAGE BUSINESS RETURN COST by program				
ALL REGISTRATIONS (Business Reply)	.40 plus postage			
WALK PLEDGE MONEY RETURN ENVELOPE	.60 (note: depends on weight — average cost to return $)			
BULK RATE	.11	UP TO THREE AND ONE-HALF OUNCES		
POSTCARD	.20			
1st CLASS FIRST OUNCE	.32			
1st CLASS SUBSEQUENT OUNCES	.23			
* BUSINESS REPLY	.40 plus postage			
ADDRESS CORRECTION REQUESTED	.50			

* NOTE: Use business reply envelopes (pre-paid postage) with caution. It is very expensive per reply. Most people participating in a cause-related event will not mind using a stamp to register. However, always use business reply envelopes for pledge return.

(Exhibit 4.1 *continued*)

"night crawl" (a walk at night), you will need to add special temporary lighting and, perhaps, additional security to this budget.

As I mentioned in the introduction, keep your eye on the big picture, but don't forget the itty-bitty details — details such as the cost of the insurance and gasoline for the rental trucks, garbage bags for clean-up, toilet paper for the port-a-potties, generators for the music, signs for registration, "address correction re-

TRAVEL				BUDGET FOR YEAR	
ACCOUNTING NUMBER:					
	SIZE	OTHER UNIT	PRICE PER UNIT	NUMBER OF UNITS	TOTAL COST
DESCRIPTION					
BROCHURE DISTRIBUTION					
TOLLS					
PARKING					
CABS					
BUSES					
PLANE FARES					
TRAIN FARES					
AUTO MILEAGE					
TOLLS					
AUTO RENTAL-NON EVENT DAY					
HOTEL ROOMS					
MEALS					

(Exhibit 4.1 *continued*)

quested" return postage costs, etc. The budget is one area where every detail *counts*. An example of one of the most overlooked details in budgeting is direct mail. A simple oversight in the direct mail budget can significantly impact profitability. For example, most of us know that if we have 10,000 brochures being mailed (first class) @ $.32 each, we must include this $3,200 expense in our budget in the "postage" account. Often, however, the *result*

EQUIPMENT RENTAL					BUDGET FOR YEAR			
ACCOUNTING NUMBER:_____								
DESCRIPTION	SIZE	OTHER UNIT	PRICE PER UNIT	NUMBER OF UNITS	CHICAGO	GREATER PEORIA	CENTRAL JOLIET	TOTAL COST
TENTS								
CHAIRS								
TABLES								
POTTIES								
TRUCKS								
VANS								
AUTOS (WHEN NEEDED)								
REFRIGERATED TRUCK								
GENERATORS								
HEATERS								
OTHERS								

(Exhibit 4.1 *continued*)

of this mailing — the postage-paid return registrations forms — have not been budgeted for, resulting in heavy non-planned expenses that must be incurred. (By the way, I don't recommend using business reply for the return of registration forms. It is costly and the majority of people will not mind using one of their own stamps. In fact, I tested the response rate of stamped by donor versus pre-paid replies — the response was nearly 50 to 50!) Regardless, make sure to go over your budget with a

PROGRAM SUPPLIES [   ]   BUDGET FOR YEAR [   ]

ACCOUNTING NUMBER:_____

DESCRIPTION	SIZE	OTHER UNIT	PRICE PER UNIT	NUMBER OF UNITS	TOTAL COST
BALLOONS					
INDIVIDUAL					
ARCHES					
MARKERS					
POSTERS					
PAPER CUPS					
PLATES					
GARBAGE BAGS					
PAPER TOWELS					
TOILET PAPER					
FORKS					
SPOONS					
KNIVES					
BROCHURE HOLDERS					
RUNNER BIBS					

(Exhibit 4.1 *continued*)

fine-tooth comb — search for hidden expenses. And always look at the real cost of the event. Allocate staff time as an expense. Let's say, for example, you must pay your data entry staff at overtime rates to keep on top of the registrations coming in. This is a cost which must be planned and accounted for. Often, we are fooling ourselves as to how much an event "costs" us. If we are not careful, the event which appeared on the surface to be a star producer may drain profitability.

| Equipment Rental | **Budget Tracking Form** |

Account Number

Budget | $10,000

Date	Vendor	Items Ordered	Cost per Item	Total Cost	Cumulative	Equipment Budget	Budget Remaining
9/6	Party Time	one 10x10 tent	150	150	150	10,000	$9,850
9/7	Jay's Fence	700 sq. ft temp. fence	700	700	850	10,000	$9,150
9/8	Waste Mgt.	100 potties	40	4,000	4,850	10,000	$4,300
9/10	Halls Rentals	4,000 chairs	100	4,000	8,850	10,000	$1,150

Budget for Equipment	
Total Spent for a Year	
Total Equipment Budget of 1995	
Equipment Rentals (over or under budget)	

Note: You'll want to create separate pages for every account number, e.g., postage, supplies, etc. See the sample budget, exhibit 4.1, on for specific account categories.

(Exhibit 4.2) A budget tracking form can save you a lot of time when you need to know how your organization's money is being spent.

Statistics and Projecting Your Financial Objectives

Let's take a look at some key statistical indicators of gross profit as a percentage of gross income in the table below. It tells us that gross profit as a percentage of gross income varies from 66% in 1994 to 71% in 1993. Conversely, gross expense as a percentage of gross income (expense ratio) varies 29% in 1993 to 34% in 1994.

Gross Profit as a Percentage of Gross Income: "The Fun Walk"

Description	1995	1994	1993
Gross income	100%	100%	100%
Gross expense as a % of gross income	31%	34%	29%
Gross profit as a % of gross income	69%	66%	71%

What does this mean? It tells you your gross profit will be at any level of gross income. Since gross income is always 100%, all we have to do is estimate a gross income dollar amount and we can compute the gross expense and gross profit. In 1995 the gross expense as a percentage of gross income is 31% and the gross profit as a percentage of gross income is 69%. If gross income is $2,000,000 dollars, then gross expense is $620,000 dollars and you have a gross profit of $1,380,000.

The calculation for gross profit is: multiply the estimated gross income in dollars by the gross profit as a percentage of gross income. Therefore, you multiply the $2,000,000 (estimated gross income) by .69 (because 69% is the gross profit as a percent of gross income) and you arrive at a gross income in dollars of $1,380,000.

The gross profit looks good, but now we must deduct fixed costs from the gross income. **Fixed costs** are those expenses that do not vary with volume in any significant amount. The salary and fringe benefits for the campaign manager are generally considered fixed costs because they will be there whether you have 100 or 10,000 walkers.

The table of pledge averages shows us that participants are optimistic at the time they make their pledge. Note that the pledge amount is higher than the amount paid.

Pledge Averages

Description	1995	1994	1993
Pledged	$84.00	$86.00	$98.00
Paid	$76.00	$75.00	$86.00

Based on this data, let's do an exercise. First, how much of a net profit do you want to make? Let's say a cool million. Yes, that's right, $1,000,000 after all income adjustments and expenses. Here we go. (Some of the following amounts are rounded to the nearest whole dollar for simplicity.)

1. Determine the formula for the model.

Again, let's assume we want to net $1,000,000. Gross profit percentage is 69%, and the fixed costs are $50,000.

    a. Gross Income = gross profit + gross expense
    b. Fixed Expenses = $50,000 (a given)
    c. Net Profit = $1,000,000 (a given)
    d. Gross Profit = 69% of gross income (a given)
    e. Gross Expense = 31% of gross income (a given)

2. Use the formula.

Description	Amount	% of Gross Income
Gross Income	$1,521,739	100%
Less Gross Expense	$ 471,739	31%
Gross Profit	$1,050,000	69%
Less Fixed Expenses	$ (50,000)	
Net Profit	$1,000,000	

3. Explain the numbers.

This is how we got there: The gross profit is equal to the net profit plus the fixed expenses: $1,050,000 = $1,000,000 + $50,000

To determine gross income you divide gross profit by the given gross profit as a percent of gross income: **When gross profit ($1,050,000) is divided by 69% (gross profit as a percentage of gross income) = $1,521,739 gross income.**

To determine gross expense you multiply gross expense as a percentage of gross income by gross income: **When gross income ($1,521,739) is multiplied by 31% (gross expense as a percentage of gross income) = $ 471,739 gross expense.**

The Concepts in the Model

The model assumes that gross income, gross expense and gross profit are variable. Variable in that at any volume of participants, the net profit remains the same. Therefore, whether you have 100 walkers or 10,000 walkers the net profit remains the same. Let's assume that 15,000 participants walked in the event in the above example (we should all be so lucky!). That means that each walker brought in an average of $101.45 in pledges. The calculation: Gross income per participant divided by the number of participants. $1,521,739 ÷ 15,000 = $101.45. This allows us to use the formula on any level of anticipated gross income. Cost per participant is computed by dividing the gross expense by the number of participants with a resultant answer of $31.45. Therefore, gross profit per participant is $70.00 (subtract the cost per participant from the gross income per participant). Let's check the percentages of these dollar amounts: $70.00 (gross profit) divided by $101.45 (gross income) = 69% (gross profit as a percentage of gross income). Exhibit 4.3 presents this in an easily understandable table.

Variable expenses

The crucial variable expense budget requires attention to detail and control over the timing of expenditures. What kind of

Gross Profit as a Percentage
of Gross Income

# Description	Dollar Amount Column A	% to Gross Income Column B	Per participant Column C	Line #
1 Gross Income	$1,521,739	100%	$101.45	1
2 Gross Expense	–$ 471,739	– 31%	–$ 31.45	2
3 Gross Profit	$1,050,000	69%	$ 70.00	3
4 Fixed expenses	$ (50,000)	3%	$ 3.33	4
5 Net profit	$1,000,000	66%	$ 66.67	5
6 Number of participants			15,000	6

(Exhibit 4.3) Use this table to calculate your income per participant. Note that the gross expense percentage (31% of the gross income) is far too high. It should never be more than 25%.

detail, you ask? Well, to get 15,000 participants we had to mail out 150,000 pieces of direct mail, make 20,000 calls, buy 15 billboards and print 680,000 brochures — not to mention providing 13,000 prizes, snacks, etc. (You've probably guessed that these examples are fictitious and are for example only. Please do not use these numbers when figuring out your budget!)

Exhibit 4.4 shows these and other variable expenses. Each variable expense budget is different in terms of the number of categories of expense. The overall idea with variable expenses is that you must get into those details. It will be grueling work at times, but it will save you a lot of grief in the end and enhance your bottom line.

As we said in the preceding chapter, "plan your work and work your plan." Know the details like the back of your hand and

Variable Expense Budget Example

Variable expense summary	Amount
Postage	$ 25,705
Billboards	25,000
Prizes	320,000
Trucks	2,200
Food	34,000
Balloons	600
Tents	5,000
Telemarketers	42,000
Telephone	6,000
Contingency	11,234
Total Variable Expense	$471,739

Variable expense detailed description

Postage		Date	Rate	units	Amount
1st mailing		01-March			
	bulk		0.11	20,000	$ 2,200
	regular		0.28	1,000	280
	special		0.45	1,000	450
2nd mailing		01-April			
	bulk		0.11	20,000	2,200
	regular		0.28	2,500	700
	special		0.45	2,500	1,125
FedX regular	Prizes	15-May	1.25	15,000	18,750
Total Postage					$ 25,705

Billboards	various	1666.64	15	25,000
Prizes	01-June	20.00	16,000	320,000
Trucks	15-April	220.00	10	2,200
Food	19-April	2.00	17,000	34,000
Balloons	19-April	.6	1,000	600
Tents	19-April	5.00	1,000	5,000
Telemarketers	28-March	5.25	8,000	42,000
Telephone	various			6,000
Contingency	insurance			11,234
				$471,739

(Exhibit 4.4) This variable expense budget gives you an idea of the kinds of expenses you should take into consideration in your budget. Note that these amounts are for example only and do not reflect real costs or recommendations.

incorporate them into the budget. Have two or three colleagues check your plan for reasonableness. Don't forget to have an accountant review and recalculate your figures.

Computer Systems

From the time I write this book to the time it is published, computer hardware and software will have changed in some significant way. Naturally, there is no single system that is flexible enough to accommodate all types and sizes of nonprofits. In assessing systems needs, one must address the following factors: flexibility, integration and expandability. These may be obvious, yet they remain key factors in a needs assessment. Obviously, the main factor will be the size of the organization. Certainly a national organization with branch offices and event participation in the tens of thousands will have different computer needs than a local community organization holding an annual event that attracts less than 300 participants. However, fundamentally the approach to addressing systems needs are the same. Therefore, I will remain general in my discussion of the subject.

One key to upgrading a present system or installing a new system is utilizing the assistance of a computer professional/expert. First, look to your board members. It is very likely that one or more have in-house computer analysts on staff within their own corporations. Board members may consider "loaning" this individual for a special project. Other good sources of knowledgeable people and state-of-the-art technology are universities — universities often look for special computer projects for graduate students. Call up the head of the department and explain your situation. Your specific niche (pledge-based event) is often the challenge they look for when selecting a project for graduate students. Projects are always supervised by professors, ensuring the best advice around.

I have been fortunate to have been associated with nonprofits which are fairly sophisticated in information systems — including on-site systems analysts and customized systems. Most nonprofits, however, do not have these luxuries. Through my experience working with and managing systems, I have learned what I believe to be the most important factor in systems: the ability to track — participants, donations, zip codes, direct mail, etc. Tracking enables you to reach new markets and to make the entire process more efficient, especially in streamlining registration. Through tracking you will have the ammunition to scientifically plan for growth by analyzing your data. When making decisions on the type of software and in the design of the databases, you must think in terms of flexibility and future growth. When looking at software, look at development capability, soundness/reliability of company, obtain user testimony, integration capabilities with other software packages, platform (what kind of hardware it needs to run on) and, most of all, technical support.

In assessing software needs, look at the size of your organization or the size of your event and the expected number of participants, as well as the number of records you'll want to capture in the database. Some store-bought software packages, such as Access or Approach, may be adequate for your organization's needs. However, custom software may be more appropriate if you have several large events per year with multiple participant databases.

Important Data to Capture:

1. Personal information (name, address, phone)
2. Relationship to organization
3. How participant heard about event
4. Is the participant a veteran, i.e., walked in this event before?
5. Specifics of the event, e.g., route location, etc.
6. Prize selection, t-shirt size, etc.
7. Amount pledged
8. Amount paid
9. Is participant a team member?
10. Little nuances — whatever need you might have for your *unique* event (this could change from year to year)

One key to a successful event is pleasing the participants, making them feel their participation and contribution make a difference by giving them specialized and efficient treatment. As I have mentioned and will mention continually throughout the book is the fact that *individuals who have participated before cost less to recruit and raise more money.* Systems can help increase your participants' satisfaction with your event. A quick response to inquiries, fast and simple registration, personalized direct mail and quick post-event follow-up are all ways in which systems can help you achieve your goal. These all make lasting impressions on participants and often affect their future participation (and their recommendation to others).

Systems Do's:

- ✓ Allow past participants to call in registrations over the phone.
- ✓ Set up systems so that staff fielding walk calls can take the information over the phone and enter directly into systems, avoiding handwriting errors and lost potential participants.
- ✓ Use laptops for registration at the event (if sponsored).
- ✓ Send personalized letters to top fund raisers (more on this later).
- ✓ Use systems to track prizes and inventory (if prize fulfillment is done in-house). Good prize inventory systems can save money and make re-ordering more efficient.

It is paramount that the computer system you put in place for your event be able to integrate and/or transfer data into your accounting system. This will make your organization more efficient and will maintain data integrity and decrease errors.

Five

Making Your Cause Compelling

You have a population of folks whom you know personally. They may have a physical handicap or they're hungry or homeless ... or, you work for an environmental organization, like the Jewish National Fund, and your mission is to build infrastructures, dams and reservoirs in Israel to help provide the much-needed water. Regardless of your mission, you've seen the struggle — perhaps emotionally, physically, politically and/or financially. You want to help ... badly. Besides, it's your job. You want to let everyone out there know about your cause and its need for financial support — or research, respite, treatment and shelter in the case of health related organizations or, in the case of non-health-related causes, saving the rain forest, fighting for peace. No matter what the reason, it's natural to sometimes — naively — place these individuals and/or causes in the worst possible light; to use adjectives to describe their situation, like ravaging, devastating, terminal, that make their plight sound hopeless. Or, worse still, to show individuals — in particular — in compromising positions. Whatever the disease or cause, as development professionals we must avoid sinking into this perilous pit. It's too easy. Yes, it's tempting, but the consequences can be dangerous. For the most part, though, I think we're doing a respectable job in this area. However, there is always room for improvement. Before I get to the strategies involved in creating a memorable name and image and the importance of tag-lines, I would be doing our fund-raising community a disservice if I didn't share some of the consequences of sensational pleas:

Many years ago I participated on a national walk task team, comprised of the top 10 revenue-producing chapters out of 400+ walk sites. Our goal was simple: to re-name and/or re-evaluate our walk's name. But along the way — as I'm sure you've found in this type of discussion — we discovered something far more prophetic than reviewing the actual name. We learned how important it was to our "clients" (people who had the disease that we were fighting were called "clients") that they be portrayed in the most positive way.

For most of us, whether raising money for individuals with a disease or for causes such as homelessness or the environment, we must keep in mind the *greater* impact and/or future repercussions. By this, I'm referring to what I call **secondary consequences.** For example, I once saw a highly controversial ad that showed a man entangled in chains. It even went so far as to suggest that this person might sound as if he had marbles in his mouth when speaking. This advertisement was not well received because not everyone who gets the disease reacts in the same way — in fact, the majority of people living with this particular disease will *never* experience *any* of these symptoms. Perhaps this exploitive ad generated attention . . . but at what cost? A secondary consequence of this type of advertising might be that potential employers may worry about hiring a person with this "ravaging" disease or firing ones that already work for them. And, as I'm sure you can imagine and have experienced, the biggest consequence is the loss of good will and respect of one's own "clients" and/or donors.

One thing we will talk about later on is recruitment from your constituents or members. And especially in health-related events, one of the best recruitment sources is one's own mailing list of affected people *and their family and friends.* As you may have already learned through doing events, although people living with a disease may not be able to actually participate, they have family, friends, co-workers and neighbors who can. How much more money do these people raise than a person not tied to the disease of a cause raise? Let me give you an idea: The top 10 fund raisers in the last walk I organized were: 1 husband, 2 wives, 1 sister, 1 brother, 1 mother and father and 4 people with the disease (1 out of the 4 did not participate). One of my closest friends, Kathy D., lives with multiple sclerosis in Denver. While she has successfully completed the walk in years past, she recently has collected greater amounts *not* participating. She simply sent out a letter asking people to sponsor her even though she isn't participating. Bike tour top fund-raiser numbers are similar, but generally speaking cyclists are not quite as loyal to the cause — they are similar to runners; sometimes the thrill of the competition overrides their altruism. Due to the high cost of equipment associated with a long distance cycling event, I recommend requiring at least a $25 registration fee for a one-day event and a $35 fee for a two-day tour — *with a minimum pledge amount of $100 to $200*. Most running races have a small entry fee of $10 to $15, give a t-shirt and do not get mixed up in incentives. If they do, it's purely a secondary deal.

What's in a Name?

Now that you've pinpointed compelling reasons for people to participate, it's time to take all the information and create a name for the event.

What's in a name? It's simply not good enough to be an organization that saves lives or helps the environment or the homeless — you must also be able to project your organization's mission through its name. Not having the budget to hire a creative person is no excuse for poor marketing. We all have access to savvy marketers and information, we just need to find the resources and use them. Again, we must run our event like a successful business.

Some organizations have the good fortune to have the counsel of an advertising firm. If your organization doesn't, begin now to cultivate contacts within this arena. The best tip I learned is to get young, creative types or junior account executives on any junior boards you may have. These young future executives often have access to great talent as well as production. (As we know too well, hiring the firm itself is usually too expensive for most non-profits.) These people often get others within different departments involved. Soon, it's not long before top-rate work is done gratis. And another *phenomenal* benefit not often looked at is sponsorship opportunities. Often these individuals are working with top accounts, and other young professionals on their way up are working on the other side for consumer product companies likely to have big budgets for cash and in-kind donations. It's wonderful if you can nab some hot professional who has already made it. But — especially in advertising where the life of a job in an agency is often less than two years — don't count on continuity or loyalty to your cause if the person you worked with leaves. This is why I strongly recommend cultivating young professionals. If you are lucky enough to tap into the top echelons of an agency, great, but if not, I recommend starting at the "bottom" of a large agency or going to a small operation.

Here's a short story about a near name tragedy. In my infinite wisdom, I thought I could come up with a new name for an event all by myself. And I did. I thought it was brilliant: the "Great Lakes Getaway Bike Tour." Catchy, right? I thought we were destined for another great event. Final destination: Lake Geneva, Wisconsin. Theoretically, the tour would pass many *Illinois and Wisconsin lakes* (hence "Great Lakes"). The name was soon to be printed on a mere *250,000* brochures. Quite by accident, I proudly mentioned the name to some colleagues, expecting praise for my new creation. Molly Quinn, former president and CEO of Sportcorp, a sporting event management and consulting firm based in Chicago, asked me where in *Michigan* did this event go? Puzzled, I replied, *"Michigan?* The event is in *Illinois,* not Michigan!" I soon realized that the phrasing "Great Lakes" implied *the* Great Lakes (Erie, Superior, etc.). The situation was quickly remedied (thankfully before the 250,000 brochures went to print) by simply deleting the "s" at the end of Lakes, i.e., "The Great Lake Getaway," implying *Lake* Geneva, *Wisconsin,* a vacation hot spot and our final destination.

Whether you have access to creative talent or not, the following is the best strategy I've seen for the creation of a name. You know your mission better than anyone else ever could. I recommend you investing the time in this group process. This has been such an invaluable resource for creating a name.

Involve the Decision Maker

In my quest for methods for creating names, I asked many ad agency people and market researchers who was the best idea person around. A man by the name of Fred Meyer, president of Ideas To Go, Inc., was mentioned several times. Here's the strategy Fred uses to come up with good, compelling names for events:

> It really isn't hard to generate names. What's difficult is getting agreement. The evaluation of names is one of the most subjective activities you'd ever hope to find. It's so easy for someone to look at a list of prospective names and say, "Nice try, but none of these really turn me on." On the other hand, if someone has a sweat equity in both generating names and evaluating them in terms of what's right about them, he or she is more likely to appreciate the names' value. For that reason, we encourage you to always to get the decision makers involved in helping to create names and/or doing a constructive evaluation of them.

Put together a team of six to 10 people to participate in a name generation meeting. Select people who need to be there for political reasons and people who are good with words. Have one person serve as facilitator/recorder.

Get one or more easels with big sheets of paper on which to write the names as they are generated. Use water-based markers to avoid show-through on the paper and to keep the recorder from "permanent" stains. Have small pads and pencils for each participant.

Three Easy Steps to Creating a Good Name

Here are ways to create a name that will help you reach your target market:

1. *Identify what the names might communicate.*

Build a list of "what's true" about the event. What is the activity? What is the cause being supported? Who will the participants be? Besides contributing to a cause, what's in it for participants or spectators? Where will it be held? When? What's special about it? List as many answers to these questions as you can come up with.

2.   *Select the most important things that the name could communicate.*

Look at the situation from the viewpoint of a prospective participant or sponsor. Will they be interested in the fun of the event? Or in feeling good about helping with the cause? Or in the satisfaction of a difficult achievement? Is the identity of the beneficiary of the event important? Is civic pride an issue? These are the kinds of things you might consider as *opportunities* for focus in name generation.

3.   *Brainstorm name possibilities to reflect the opportunities you've selected.*

Alex Osborne, the father of brainstorming, set these rules for the process:

(a) *Criticism is ruled out.* Adverse judgment of ideas must be withheld until later. (This is the most important of the rules because it makes it safe to contribute ideas without fear of criticism.)

(b) *"Free wheeling" is welcomed.* The wilder the idea, the better; it is easier to tame down than to think up.

(c) *Quantity is wanted.* The greater the number of ideas, the more the likelihood of good ideas.

(d) *Combinations and improvements are necessary.* In addition to contributing ideas of their own, participants should suggest how ideas of others can be turned into better ideas or how two or more ideas can be joined into still another idea.

Those rules, first published in 1953 in the book *Applied Imagination,* still work beautifully today.*

Applied Imagination, Alex F. Osborn, Charles Scribner's Sons, New York, 1953.

Names can be categorized in many ways. To provide some examples, let's assume a group is looking for a name for a 50-mile canoe race to be conducted on the Rum River in Minnesota on behalf of Camp Hamilton, an outdoor camping experience for handicapped children. Here are some kinds of names you might seek:

- *Straightforward labels.* 50-mile Paddle for Kids, The Rum River Classic, The Camp Hamilton Down River Race.
- *Names that achieve memorability from rhyme, alliteration, puns, etc.* The Rum River Rush, The Brace Races, The Rum Runners 50, Tippy Canoes and Dollars, Too.
- *Phonetic spellings.* Qwik Canooz, Kamping for Kidz Klassic.
- *Off the wall, crazy names.* I Can't Believe I Made It 50 Miles, The Achy Shaky, The "I Can. Canoe?"
- *Put two words into one coined word.* Rumathon, Canoe-athon, RumAnoo.
- *Names that suggest challenge in the event.* Look what you might do with variations on the word "endurance": The Enduro 50, The Rum Enduran. The Hamilton Endura. Endurathon. Or, Rapids Buster. 10,000 Strokes. Paddle Out of the Pack.

Remember Roget!

There's nothing like a good thesaurus when you're working on names. Not only for the synonyms, but for modifying sayings and for word parts to force together. Have three or four of them handy for your group.

When you've thought of a few hundred names evaluate them in three steps:

1. *Set some criteria for a good name.* Most lists of criteria suggest that the name should be relevant, should be appropriate to the cause and the sponsoring organization, should be easy to pronounce, and should be new and different from any competing events.
2. *Nominate the names you are for.* Don't waste time sorting out names that are disliked. Simply give each participant

a set number of nominations to make from the list. Have them build their list of nominations on their own pads first, then register their nominations on the big easel sheets with "X's" or check marks.

3. *Evaluate all of the names that received multiple nominations.* Have the participants note all of the reasons why a name is right for the event and why they could be for it. Also, allow people to champion names that they feel strongly about, even though others may not have nominated those names. Sometimes one person sees good qualities that others have missed.

Note: It is particularly important that the key decision makers take part in the evaluation process so that they come to understand the values perceived in the names and develop some ownership of the output of the session.

Develop a short list of finalists. Ten names is about the right number. Get to this number by having participants nominate a set number of names from among those that have been evaluated. Go with those that receive the most nominations.

Test Your Finalists

Try the names out on prospective participants and sponsors. Do a mini "research" project by asking 20 people who might take part in the event to pick three favorites each from the list of 10 names. Ask them why they chose the ones they did. Also ask them which one is the worst name and why.

Select Your Winner

On the basis of the research responses and your discussion, pick your winner and go with it.

In addition to Fred's wonderfully creative suggestions, I have a few additions:

1. People to ask to participate in name selection:

- The event coordinator or manager
- 1 board member
- 2 event committee members (if event has existed before)
- 1 committee member from other in-house events (especially helpful if event has not existed)
- 2 people *not* familiar with your event and/or organization
- 2–3 past participants
- The organization *receptionist* (yes, receptionist!). This individual is often the most familiar with all inner workings of the organization and has his or her finger on the pulse of your members
- 1 person from client, patient or member services
- 1 person from your finance department

2. Tell the participants as little as possible before their arrival. I prefer to tell them they are on an important "task force" for the *XYZ* event. Do not encourage any further discussion, but assure them this is going to be fun "work." Consider offering some type of "reward" for participation, e.g., an afternoon off, lunch for two, etc.

3. Meet in a large conference-type room *outside your office* in the morning, around nine a.m. works best. Board members are usually willing to share their conference room for a few hours.

After the name (and "tag-line") has been created for the event, it is imperative that it is kept "in the faces" of potential participants, that is, virtually everyone! This can be achieved through client (patient) or constituent programs, media awareness, pre-event educational materials/newsletters and should be carried on *at the event itself* — this will accomplish two very important things: First, it will help create awareness not only of your event, but of your organization; and second, it will help tie the event to your cause and your cause to the event.

Six

Communications Development

Why are communications important? Creating your communications image will:

- Set the tone of your event
- Help tie your event to your mission
- Create a lasting impression

Communications is perhaps the best way to bring nonprofit events out of that "mom and pop" arena I spoke of in the introduction. With foresight and skill, and the talent of a hired professional or creative volunteer, a powerful campaign image can take nonprofit events to the next level, thus driving recruitment. During the height of event season (depending on your market), your communication pieces may find themselves among a myriad of other pieces, all vying for participants (and pledges). You need to stand out! Most of all, you must keep that message simple. You only have a few seconds to get your prospect's attention!

Communications is the cornerstone of your recruitment and promotions plan (see Chapter 11). It is the writing, design and production of all collateral materials, including brochures, direct mail pieces and any promotional advertising. Don't even think about trying to do your communications on an as-needed basis! Just as your timeline is vital to strategic planning, the communications schedule (Exhibit 6.1) is critical to the success of your event and a necessary component in budget preparation — without the schedule, you'll be paying 10 times what you may have intended because of rushes and changes. Additionally, if you plan in advance, you can complete many of the campaign pieces well *before* the event begins, saving critical time during the planning months and possibly allowing for volume discounts in printing and paper. Also, you can avoid a possible loss in participants due to missed recruitment opportunities because materials weren't sent on time.

As you can see in the following communications schedule, there are certain elements necessary for good management and tracking. These components are: 1) completion/drop date and 2) complete description of piece, including quantity and paper stock.

Components of a Communications Campaign

Here are the main components of a communications campaign:
1. Brochure or primary recruitment piece
2. Poster
3. Registration packet
   • Welcome letter
   • Pledge sheet
   • Newsletter: how to raise pledges, logistical info, directions, info on cause, etc. (see section below)
   • Receipts
   • Matching gift list
   • Participant ID card
   • Route maps
4. Newsletters

As I've mentioned before, staying in contact with your participants year-round is the key to retention and pledge fulfillment. Many times, participants will register six months (in the case of a bike tour) before the event day. If you don't keep on psyching them up for the event and reminding them of the

Event Communications Schedule

Completion Date	Communication	Target	Quantity	Printing Needs	Method of Mailing	Responsibility	Date Completed
7 months out	Brochure and poster	Everyone	10,000/ 2,000		Bulk	Tracy	
6 months out	Event letterhead (for all communication pieces)		9,000	Bond/1c/1s		Joe	
5 months out	Event party invitation	Past year's leaders and teams and past top fund raisers	650	Card stock /1c/2 side/2 per page	First class	Joe	
5 months out	Registration packet Newsletter #1 Pledge sheets Matching gift forms Receipts Extra brochures for friend and team recruitment 9 x 12 envelope Walker I.D. card Ribbon or incentive with personalized direct mail	Registered walkers	2,500	Text/1 page/1c/2s Text/1 page/1c/2s Text/1 page/1c/2s Inventory 1c/1s Cover/1c/2s/4/page Purchased	First class	Joe	
5 months out	Pre-Event letter to past participants	Past registrants (who were no-shows)	2,500	Letterhead/1c/1s	Bulk	Joe	

(Exhibit 6.1) Here is an example of a communications schedule. Planning the development and production of your communications pieces is essential; in the long run it will save you time and money. Note that 1c equals one color; 2c equals two colors.

Event Communications Schedule

					First Class	
3 months out	Past team captain packet	Past team captains	160			Susan
	Letter			Letterhead/1c/1s		
	Captain's fact sheet			Cover/1c/1s/3/page		
	Brochure			1c/1s		
	Envelope					
	Prospective team captain packet					
	Letter			Letterhead/1c/1s		
	Captain's fact sheet			Cover/1c/1s/3/page		
	Brochure			1c/1s		
	Envelope					
	General team captain info. sheet					
	Registered team captain packet				With registration packets	
	Letter			Letterhead/1c/1s		
	Captain's fact sheet			Cover/1c/1s/3/page		
	Company memo			Text/1c/1s		
	Sign-up sheet			Text/1c/1s		
	Team captain pin			Purchased		
	Incentive			Purchased		
	Envelope			9 x 12/1c/1s		
3 months out	Member fact sheet	Registered team members	750	Text/1c/1s	With registration packets	Joe
	Member badge			Cover/1c/1s/3/page		

Event Communications Schedule

2 months out	Personalized past participant flyer	Past four years' participants	4,200	Text/1c/2s self mailer	Bulk	Tracy
2 months out	Past participant flyer #2	Past participants who have not registered	500 less than $500 in pledges (Veteran Walker Club) 100 for $500 to $999 in pledges (Elite "Feat" Club) 75 for $1000+ in pledges (Golden Toes Club)	Cover/1c/1s	Bulk	Joe
1 month out	Past participant flyer #3	Past participants who have not registered	300 less than $500 in pledges 75 for $500 - $999 in pledges 10 for $1000+ in pledges	Cover/1c/2s	Bulk	Joe

Event Communications Schedule

		Participants		Letterhead/1c/1s Purchased Text/1c/1s 1c/1s 1c/1s	Hand out event day	Joe	
1 month out	Completion packets Thank you letter Certificate Evaluation/prize form 6 x 9 return envelope 9 x 12 envelope		3,000			Joe	
1 month out	Newsletter #2	Registered walkers	2,500	Cover/2 pages/1c/2s	Bulk for pre-registered walkers	Joe	
1 week out	Walk reminder postcard	Registered walkers	2,000	Cover/1c/2s/4/page	First class	Joe	
1 week out	Prize enclosure	Walkers	2,000	Cover/1c/1s/2/page	UPS with prize	Joe	
1 day after	Chaser postcard #1	All walkers	3,000	Cover/1c/2s/4/page	Bulk	Joe	
2 weeks after	Newsletter #3 ($ results, team photos, etc.)	Participating walkers	2,500	Text/2 pages/1c/1s	Bulk/self-mailer	Joe	
5 weeks after	Chaser letter #1	Non-paying walkers	2,000	Letterhead/1c/1s	Bulk	Joe	

importance of the cause, they may lose interest (and go to a competitor). Also, year-round contact will help with participant renewal. Past participants not only raise more money, they cost a lot less to recruit and are the best recruiters (in Chapter 11 I'll talk more about the value of past participants). Event newsletters provide the perfect opportunity for pre- and post-event contact. Components of a newsletter might include:

- Letter from client
- Letter from board president
- Letter from event coordinator
- Tips for raising pledges
- Last minute event details
- Sponsor recognition
- Showcasing prizes
- Profiles of top fund raisers
- Safety tips
- Exercise tips and training programs

5. Pledge sheet

The pledge sheet is the vehicle which participants use to "sign up" sponsors. It must contain a number of important elements, such as the name of the charity, what the mission of the charity is (in simplistic terms), and a hold-harmless waiver. In addition, it should have the date when pledges are due, the event logo and much more. See Exhibit 6.2 for a sample pledge sheet.

Direct Mail Coding, Tracking and Analysis

Now that you're an expert at the logistics of direct mail (if you weren't before), it is important to *quantify* your efforts. Without measuring the results, you are simply throwing money into the wind. While initially time consuming, it is critical to put forth the effort in creating processes to measure results.

The best and simplest way in which to do this is by setting up systems to track each registration form coming in through a pre-assigned code. This can easily be done by assigning different

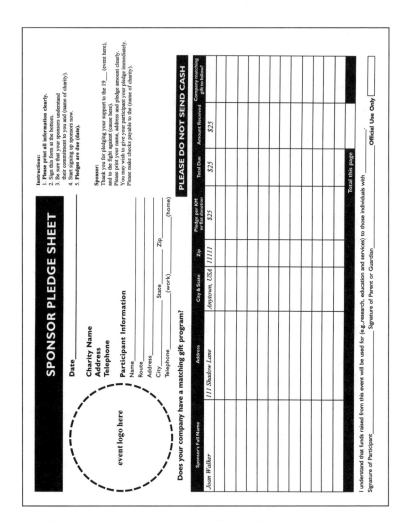

(Exhibit 6.2) Your participants should use the sponsor pledge sheet to list all of their sponsors and the amount of money they have pledged.

codes to different "groups" of mailings and/or brochures. For instance, let's say you have 10 different codes with "A" being the first "group," perhaps past participants. Let's say that you know you have 500 past participants. Therefore, you will print 500 brochures with code "A" (usually at the bottom of the registration form). A sample brochure coding form is shown in Exhibit 6.3.

Brochure Coding Form

Group	Total Number of Brochures	Code
Past participants	1,500	A
Past registrants who did not show	175	B
Top fund raisers ($500+)	200	C
Street distribution	6,000	D
Walking magazine list	4,200	E

(Exhibit 6.3) A brochure coding form tells you which brochures were sent to each market. With this coding system, you can track the results of your mailing when you receive the filled-out registration forms. In this example, 1,500 brochures were sent to past participants. All 1,500 brochures were labelled with the letter "A" at the bottom of the registration form. If you receive 500 registration forms labelled with "A," you'll know that 500 out of 1,500 (or about 33%) responded to the mailing.

This code must always be placed on your registration brochure or other registration "instrument," e.g., a flyer. When the registration form is returned, this code is right there, telling you who it came from. Naturally, this code must be entered into your computer system, which must have the capability of doing querries by that particular code. After the campaign is over, simply tally up them all and you can determine what your response rate was, the percentage of return, the average pledge that was yielded by each group, as well as the cost per thousand and the net per thousand — or hundred — mailed (see the direct mail analysis form, Exhibit 6.4). If you do not have systems in place which can do a search by code, this process is painstakingly long, but can be done by hand. If it's your first year and you do not have previous data to go by, you are basically making an investment in the future — but it is worth it. You'll be amazed at the lists which you thought would be great, yet yielded a 1% response and vice versa.

DIRECT MAIL ANALYSIS FORM

Audience Description: _e.g., past participant mailing — code A_

Mail Date: _____

Quantity: _____

Cost: _____

Projected Revenue: _____

Source Code	Pieces Mailed	Number Responses	% Return	Average Pledge	Gross Revenue	Revenue Per M (M=1,000)	Total Cost of Mailing	Net Per M
"A"	1,500	500	33%	$150	$75,000	$50	$2,300	$48.46

↑ Number of responses divided by pieces mailed

↑ Gross revenue divided by pieces mailed

↑ Gross revenue minus cost divided by pieces mailed

(Exhibit 6.4) The direct mail analysis form charts the results of your mailings and helps you evaluate their effectiveness.

Bulk Mail

Most of us are already familiar with this foe. Bulk mail is indeed a tricky friend to have. Sure, we get mail delivered at a lesser cost, but at what price? The following are some things to watch out for when using bulk mail:

- Watch your bulk mail volunteers carefully (have someone supervise them at all times). The postal regulations on bulk mail are very strict. There are very specific ways in which bulk mail must be bundled. And then there are those different-ent colored labels which must be affixed to the top of each bundle. Attend a bulk mail class. Send your volunteers and their manager to a class. It's free from the post office.
- Bulk mail is *unpredictable!* It can be delivered the next day after its delivery to the post office, or it can take up to three weeks! Mail all time-critical pieces *first class!*
- Be careful when mailing bulk during the holidays. Those nonprofit bulk mail bags will get tossed aside!

U.S. Postal Regulations

Just as with bulk mail, it is very important to know exactly what U.S. postal regulations are *at the time you are doing your mailings.* Just as it is important to be sure to label your bulk mail properly or it will be sent back, you must be up to date on postal regulations. Know what you can and can't do. The worst thing in the world is to have a mass mailing printed and sent and have it returned because some small regulation wasn't followed.

As you know, it is customary to have some sort of "teaser" copy printed on the front of an envelope to attract the recipient's attention. All "teaser" copy must be placed *above* the address line. Personally, it looks odd to me, but when the post office "bar codes" your mail, your message often gets covered up. Worse yet, it could be sent back.

The Most Easily Made Postal Mistakes

- Paper too thin on self-mailers and return postcards. Paper must be mic .7 or it will be returned. Check with your printer for paper that meets this standard. That "low-cost" thin paper could end up being the most expensive paper ever, due to lost registration forms which were "eaten" up

by postal processing machines! (Believe me, I've done this myself!)
- Zip plus-four codes ignored. This will slow down your delivery or response back.
- Teaser copy or logo under delivery address line.
- You sent out a form with a business reply envelope, but you did not budget for the return of this registration form at $.40 plus postage per piece!
- Your business reply "insignia" and bar codes are not placed in the proper place.

Any printer worth his or her weight will be up on postal regulations. But don't rely on the printer. Learn the regulations yourself. Call your local post office and ask them when their next class is (they're free to the public) and/or ask them to send you their postal regulations brochure (not leisure reading!).

Brochure and Poster Design and Production

Perhaps I've put the "cart before the horse" by talking about coding and tracking of brochures and postal regulations first, but it is important to know what the pitfalls are before getting into the design and production of the brochure.

Brochure and Poster Content

Here are some crucial elements of a brochure:

- For the cover, you'll want to include the name of the event, your charity's name, and your sponsors' logos. A photo is optional.
- Inside, you should include your charity's mission, what individuals can accomplish by participating, and your 800-number to field questions about the event.
- You should also include information on the prize structure, how to form a team, a registration form (an additional

form to register a friend is optional), and a list of the event routes and distances if there is more than one.

- Don't forget to use one panel of the brochure for postal information: your charity's name and address in the upper left-hand corner; a teaser line in a spot that won't interfere with the bar coding of bulk mail; and in the upper right-hand corner, insert an indicia (the place for a stamp) to achieve bulk-rate discounts.

You will be able to easily adapt these brochure elements to any walk of any size. Remember, these are only examples; your market may have different needs. Again, you must know the demographics and psychographics of your own market to tailor the walk to your community's needs.

The poster content is usually simple. Photo. Date. Time. Place. Sponsor logos and A BIG HUGE TELEPHONE NUMBER! (An 800# is best that is hooked up to a detailed voice mail system for more information.)

Brochure (and poster) design is, in my opinion, critical. It helps bring nonprofit events out of the "mom-and-pop" arena as I spoke of in the introduction. Again, get them professionally done by someone in the graphic design field. (The same with t-shirt design or any other event merchandising you may consider offering as prizes.) One caution, however . . . occasionally you may hear from a justifiably angry person who is concerned with the cost of such a "fancy" brochure . . . you know, it's the ol' *"Why aren't you spending the money on research?"* question. I've only received this type of call a couple times. Their concern is valid. But in keeping with the BIG picture, I feel the long-term benefits far outweigh the costs. A well-done brochure will:

- Educate the public about your cause
- Tie the event to your cause
- Sell more sponsorships
- Attract more *new* participants

Brochure and Poster Production

Now, on to printers — which we all have stories about! For most purposes, you will find that a sheetfed printer is best to use for most walks and the least cost. However, if you are rolling out a national walk program or are in a large market where you will be printing hundreds of thousands of brochures, you'll want to consider a web press. Here's a quote from one of my favorite printers, Vince Lentine of Graphic Copy in Chicago, explaining the differences between web and sheetfed processes and how to choose between the two:

> To decide whether to use a web or a sheetfed press for your walk, consider the quantity, finished size and paper stock.
>
> A web press prints on a continuous roll of paper (web) at speeds over 1,500 feet per minute. The makeready or initial set-up is very costly. A web press is used for long runs. Sheetfed presses are also used for long runs, although shorter make-ready makes sheetfed better suited to short runs.
>
> The finished size of your brochure can determine when to use a web or sheetfed press. A web press has a fixed cut-off (all sheets are cut-off at the same length) and roll widths are also fixed. Sheetfed presses come in a variety of sizes and sheets are cut to fit *your* project.
>
> The types of paper available in a roll form are limited. Nearly all types of paper are made for sheetfed presses. If your walk brochure requires a fine text or cover text, chances are it would not be available on a web press.
>
> Sheetfed presses are most often used to print newsletters, brochures and corporate identity pieces. Webs are used to print large catalogs, magazines or newspapers — and jobs which are very large.

Check with a print broker first before you design your piece. He or she will best be able to tailor your needs and direct you on which way is the most cost-effective for your project. Make sure to group together a bid for all your projects for the year to negotiate a better price.

Costs vary, but naturally, the higher the print run, the lower the cost per unit. *Figure out your needs and the costs before designing that brochure!* There is no hard and fast price I can throw out because of the variety of options. Generally I recommend doing the most you can afford, especially in the infancy stage of your walk. This means bright, four-color brochures that don't get lost in the crowd. Don't forget that compelling *photo* capturing your cause and/or mission! And have the brochure *professionally designed!* Do not attempt to do this one on your home PC. Your organization's entire image is tied to this event. Once your walk has matured and you are recruiting walkers from your own past participants, your recruitment strategies will change and move away from the brochure as a registration tool. It will be replaced by other strategies, such as phone registration.

Some printers can print in two color, some can print one color. If I'm using a web press to do a four-color brochure and I'm printing 500,000, the price can be as low as $.035 cents each. However, if I'm doing a two-color sheetfed run of brochures, but only 20,000 total, I may pay $.22 cents each. So, the price, of course, is determined by many different variables, from quantity to the weight of the paper. And then there are those "codes" I told you about. The different codes assigned to each group will affect your printing costs by up to $100 per code! Why? Because each time the pressman has to stop the press (to "mask out" a code), it costs press time. The least expensive way to implement the coding process is by this "mask out" procedure in which the pressman covers up or opaques out a code, leaving the actual code as the last in a series. (See the bottom of the registration form in Exhibit 6.5 for a sample. Note that code "F" is the last code in the series. This means that this brochure came from the "F" group. Also note that there may have been several codes before this one.)

Once you have your "ducks-in-a-row" (an old Texas expression for everything ready to roll), you should be ready to start negotiations with printers, commonly known as the bidding process. Personally, it's not one of my favorite things. But I must practice what I preach and obtain at least three bids on each project. It's difficult because there's always that great person you like working with, but a new vendor comes along and knocks your old "tried and true" guy right out of there. But we all know that the least expensive doesn't always guarantee the best results. Look for the printers who have the most technical knowledge. Then ask for bids, obtain references and check them! I'm certain you've been there before. But if you haven't done pledge-based events before, you've probably never printed en masse as you will when printing walk brochures. A very rough estimate for determining the number of brochures is 60 brochures per walker your first year, 50 your next, then 40 the year after. Again, as your event

REGISTER EARLY!

Complete this form (please print) and MAIL or FAX today:
(please use ball point pen)

SPEED REGISTRATION... *You may FAX your form in anytime before April 6th to:*

Name (First)_____ (Last) _____

Phone (H) _____ (W)_____

Address _____
(no P.O. boxes, please)

City _____ State_____ Zip_____

Age _____ T-shirt size: ☐ M ☐ L ☐ XL Child: ☐ L

☐ Male ☐ Female

Employer_____

I am participating on a Team ☐ Yes ☐ No

Team Name_____

Team Captain _____

☐ I am the Team Captain ☐ A Team Member

My fund-raising goal is $ _____

My route location is: (check one)

☐ Chicago Lakefront (A) ☐ DeKalb (B) ☐ Fox Valley (C)
☐ Highland Park (D) ☐ Hyde Park (E) ☐ Joliet (F)
☐ Kankakee (G) ☐ McHenry County (H) ☐ Morris (I)
☐ Naperville (J) ☐ Oak Forest (K) ☐ Rockford (L)
☐ Schaumburg (M) ☐ Utica (N)

☐ I have walked in THE   WALK before (5V).
  Year(s) _____.

☐ Please send me _____ more brochures and a poster.
  I'll put them up at work.

☐ I will check with my company to see if they have a matching
  gifts program so I can double, even triple my pledge money!

☐ I will not be able to walk, but I would like to volunteer.
  Please send me more information.

☐ I will not be able to participate, but please accept my donation
  of $_____. (ST-D)

☐ I would like to know more about the
      Society and its programs.
  Please send more information.
      A B C D E F

(Exhibit 6.5) This registration form from an event brochure shows the codes for each mailing group. Note that there may have been several mailings before the "F" group mailing (a "G" mailing, an "H" mailing, an "I" mailing, etc.).

matures and you have a larger pool of past walkers to pull from, your brochure needs will be less. *This is a crude estimate. Every market is different. If this is your first year, track your results and plan accordingly for next year. Naturally, more is always better than less (except, of course, in terms of the cost!). Having to reprint 500 brochures is always more expensive per piece than the initial printing of 5,000! Your costs may double!*

One final note: Although I spoke of the brochure as the recruitment and registration vehicle, you may consider using your pledge sheet as your registration form. Many organizations do this. It's not as attractive and it doesn't have as much room for educating the public about the cause and current research. But it's generally less expensive. Another option is a flyer — a flyer is usually used in small walks where 200 or fewer participants are to be recruited.

Determining the Number of Brochures to Order

Unless you've gone through a walk before and have ordered brochures, there is no easy way to determine the *exact* number of brochures you'll need beforehand. Most often you'll end up with a few hundred extra in direct mail or in street distribution or a couple hundred extra that were set aside for team recruitment — or there's always that mailing that never got out. The best way to determine how many brochures you'll need is to simply list all the possible uses. Here are a few:

- Street distribution
- Direct mail (total all direct mail pieces, including a brochure)
- All cross-promotion within the organization (other events, other mailings in which you have included a brochure, etc.)
- Sponsor companies
- Team packets
- Office stock
- Office stock for teams only
- Mailings to health clubs and park districts
- Press kit brochures

- Leafleting
- Miscellaneous

I probably don't need to remind you to overestimate. As I said earlier, reprinting of brochures and/or posters is very costly because of the reduced quantity.

Seven

Volunteer Recruitment, Training and Management

Recruiting Committee Volunteers

How to Find and Cultivate Committee Volunteers

As we all know, volunteers are the life-blood of any non-profit — and are the wave of the future of nonprofits. Don't ask yourself, "Why would anyone want to volunteer?" Ask "Why wouldn't they want to?" Volunteers get a lot out of working on an event. They often attain self-respect, admiration and fulfillment. The more you have, the more outreach you have into your community. And never base the worth or commitment of a volunteer solely on an individual's educational level or position in life. One of the most committed volunteers I've worked with was a trucker named Kenny. Kenny enjoyed being on the walk committee so much he expanded his involvement to our bicycle tours, too. By the third year he had convinced the company he worked for to warehouse all our supplies, including food.

We want our committee to generally reflect our community and our target market. Cultivating CEOs as committee volunteers in a blue-collar town may not be a great match. How do we find the right volunteers? How do we cultivate them?

Committee volunteers are usually in front of our face, waiting to be *asked.* I can't tell you the number of committee volunteers who have been there but I didn't see them. But I must admit, an equal number have been *cultivated.* How do we cultivate people without exploiting or patronizing them?

I believe in cultivating a committee volunteer the way one might cultivate a friendship, by being available, trustworthy, open and honest — and always showing appreciation; this will breed enthusiasm and a greater desire to help. I'm certainly not suggesting that we become friends with our committee volunteers. I have developed some lovely friendships through committees I have worked with, but I generally don't recommend it. We are not their friends, *although we must be friendly.* For the same reason it would be difficult to have a friend as an employee, it is equally difficult to manage a volunteer who is a friend.

Look at everyone as potential cultivatees — from that vendor who supplies your paper to the UPS delivery person.

Cultivation is a year-round process — don't forget about that volunteer a month after the event is over. Plan *personalized* direct mail to committee volunteers in your year-round timeline; better yet, handwrite notes. I always respected former president George Bush for writing personal notes. Sure, we don't have time to do it, but the recipient appreciates it tenfold. And, as you know from past experience, there are often negative consequences to sending *form* acknowledgments to volunteers, especially committee volunteers you have built a relationship with. Also, plan personal calls throughout the year. Put your committee volunteers on your holiday list.

Of course, before we cultivate, we must *find and recruit* our volunteers.

Let's begin with places to find committee volunteers. Here are my recommendations on who makes the best committee volunteers and how to contact them:

- **All past fund raisers who raised over $250.** Through *personalized* direct mail.

- **Past top 10 fund raisers.** A personal call is a must.
- **Past top 10 team captains.** Again, a personal call.
- **Past participants (who paid their pledge).** Always have a section at the bottom of your event evaluation form which asks: If you are interested in participating on an event committee next year, please fill out the form below (ask for name, address, company, and phone numbers). People who send them in (even with negative comments or suggestions) are more likely to be committed — they cared enough to fill out the evaluation — and "sign up." I have not only cultivated many committee members through this method, but two major sponsorships. One through a walker who worked for a top-rated radio station and one who was the secretary of the CEO of a major boxed juice provider.
- **Sponsors.** Many sponsors become very involved in their sponsorship and look for ways to gain more "control" in the event. As I mentioned in the introduction, sponsors are doing "strategic philanthropy"; they give to get. This is the real world. Of course, there is always that great human being, the one who is purely altruistic. If you get a sponsor who is this type, hold onto him or her! Also, sponsor employees make fabulous committee volunteers.
- **Board members.** Although this is tricky, I've seen it work. I prefer to involve the board in other ways, but if they are eager, let them in.
- **City/park district workers.** These are *the best* volunteers I have ever seen! Generally, people involved in municipal work not only have access to permits, street closing information, etc., but they are often great planners, especially with logistics and safety. (I almost forgot: they know lots of folks and can greatly impact day-of volunteer numbers. *Cultivate these people!*
- **Secretaries to executives of Fortune 500 companies.** Secretaries make great committee volunteers. Their bosses are usually the ones asked to sit on charity boards. They are typically very smart, savvy and efficient people. And, as you know, it doesn't hurt that they have great *access* to many other contacts within their organization.

- **Union people.** Yes, union guys (and gals). They are spirited and have loads of contacts you wouldn't believe — from bus drivers to city officials.
- **Past top donors to your organization.** Review old records. If you have a sophisticated systems network, query up all the people who gave at least X amount in the past two consecutive years.

In the case of health-related nonprofits, look toward your members (patients, clients, etc.) and their families. Spouses make great committee volunteers.

Committee/Subcommittee Structure

Recruiting a Committee Chair

The chair of a committee should begin at least seven months prior to a walk and at least ten months for a long-distance cycling event. The ideal candidate for chair is someone who is already a community leader, is well-connected, and has a tie or commitment to your cause and mission. However, if this caliber person is not available, the event manager must assume this role. In the case of multiple sites/routes, the site manager should assume this role. I must admit, I assumed this role quite a few times. But in order to expand the organization and our volunteer base, we must cultivate, then delegate!

Organizing the Committee

I generally do not like to get the committee involved until after the staff leaders of the event have gotten together and have made basic decisions (date, time, place), usually about three or four months "out" (three months *before* event day). However, there is no "right" time to begin meeting . . . there are many variables, e.g., your market, staff, community resources and most of all, the *type* of event. In the case of long-distance cycling events you will want to involve route design volunteers as early as 10 months before the event because most cycling events include information about the route in the brochure. At this point, let's assume you have your master event timeline. Review the timeline and see what you and your staff want to keep and what you think you can "give away" — although never, never give away anything completely! (More on this shortly.) There are many components to any successful event; I recommend building subcommittees (with two or three people each, one being a subcommittee chair) around five areas (see committee structure chart in Exhibit 7.1):

1. Recruitment — identify, recruit and cultivate participants.
2. Sponsorship — solicit and secure in-kind and cash sponsorships to offset event expenses.
3. Logistics — help coordinate route, medical, communications, signs, registration, transportation and safety. (It is important to get input of participants, especially in the case of long-distance bicycle tours. For walks, the route can often be determined by staff.)
4. Publicity/promotion — coordinate event media campaign with internal PR staff (if you have them). Committee volunteers are usually very helpful in the areas of pre-event promotions and day-of entertainment.
5. Volunteer recruitment — recruit volunteers to help in office as well as the day of the event.

Sharing Ownership . . . Without Giving Up Control!

This is arguably one of the most difficult things to do in committee management. It is truly an art form. Quite frankly, I'm still learning to do this gracefully. I was fortunate to have a wonderful mentor in this area. Benita Shobe, currently vice president of human resources for the National Leukemia Society, taught me how to share ownership . . . by her example. As a young and naive special event coordinator, Benita gave me a lot of responsibility, strict deadlines and lots of praise. Most of all, she always

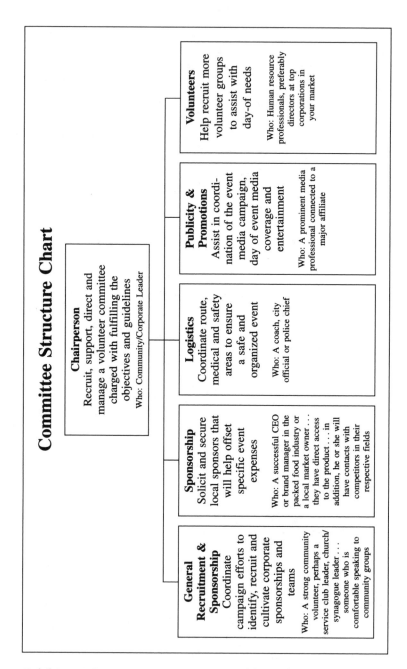

Committee Structure Chart

Chairperson
Recruit, support, direct and manage a volunteer committee charged with fulfilling the objectives and guidelines
Who: Community/Corporate Leader

General Recruitment & Sponsorship
Coordinate campaign efforts to identify, recruit and cultivate corporate sponsorships and teams
Who: A strong community volunteer, perhaps a service club leader, church/synagogue leader . . . someone who is comfortable speaking to community groups

Sponsorship
Solicit and secure local sponsors that will help offset specific event expenses
Who: A successful CEO or brand manager in the packed food industry or a local market owner . . . they have direct access to the product . . . in addition, he or she will have contacts with competitors in their respective fields

Logistics
Coordinate route, medical and safety areas to ensure a safe and organized event
Who: A coach, city official or police chief

Publicity & Promotions
Assist in coordination of the event media campaign, day of event media coverage and entertainment
Who: A prominent media professional connected to a major affiliate

Volunteers
Help recruit more volunteer groups to assist with day-of needs
Who: Human resource professionals, preferably directors at top corporations in your market

(Exhibit 7.1) Organize committees around the elements in this chart, and make sure that your chair is updated regularly about the progress of each committee.

let me *feel* I owned the event — not only allowing me to make mistakes and deal with the consequences, but also allowing me to bask in the success of many events. Looking back, however, she never relinquished control. She didn't need to, because she set strict timelines and *expected detailed updates.* I encourage everyone to try this approach with your volunteers and staff.

Managing Committees and Developing Leaders

Now that you've secured a committee and set up a committee/subcommittee structure, how do you manage them? My first suggestion is to do just that — manage. Similar to the way one manages his/her employees, you must manage your volunteers. Let them know that this is a synergistic team and each and every person is an important cog in the wheel; if one person doesn't follow through on an important responsibility, it affects the group. Let them know what you expect up front. Give them responsibility. *Trust them* — and if it doesn't come out right the first time, let them try again. Help them see the BIG picture. Set boundaries. Set deadlines. Make sure there are consequences if deadlines are not met. Naturally, "firing" difficult or unmotivated volunteers is not an option (except in very extreme cases), but *reassigning* them is. Don't scare volunteers, just make sure they understand the rules. If there is a chance a volunteer could jeopardize a potential relationship with a past sponsor, don't allow them to make "the ask." Or, if there is a person who is new to the area and has never participated in a walk, it probably isn't a good idea to assign him or her to route planning. Just as it is important to create a demographic match with sponsors, it is equally important here.

One last important *don't* on the management of volunteers: After you've promoted teamwork, don't limit your recognition to the chairperson (this applies to staff and team captains as well). Make sure recognition is given to everyone in the same way.

Just as a jury foreman (foreperson?) rises to the ranks within a matter of hours at a trial, future leaders reveal themselves soon, too. Following are a few tips on how to spot a leader:

- Accepts and often seeks out responsibilities beyond what is assigned;
- Takes pride in his or her work, and shows a personal commitment to quality;
- Is a team player;
- Is eager to learn more about the cause;
- Can be trusted; and
- Is open to constructive criticism.

Now that we've identified leaders, how do we develop them?

Recognition and Motivation

Volunteers are like gold — clearly your most valuable asset. Without them, the cost of a walk would become prohibitive. While a simple follow-up, such as a personalized "thank you" letter, is all that is expected, an extra-special recognition goes a long way to retaining that volunteer and motivating him/ her to do more the next year (or next *event*). Again, this is all about cultivation. It is especially important to thank committee volunteers; they not only work three to 10 months pre-event, but they are often the ones out there with you at five a.m. helping set up. Further, the more history a volunteer has with your event, the more ownership he/she takes. The more the volunteer "owns" the event, the more committed he/she is and the more motivated to not only continue the following year, but increase involvement. Below are ways in which to thank your committee (mix and match depending upon committee size, budget and community):

- T-shirt and sweatshirt.
- Public thank you on event day.
- Special name tags and/or ribbons identifying committee members.
- Post-event party for committee volunteers only. (Host in your home or ask a bank to host in their facility — they need not be sponsors. And banks often have private dining areas for executives.)
- Personalized, hand-written thank you on special cards.

- Thank you in walk newsletter, perhaps with photos.
- News releases to each volunteer's "hometown" newspaper announcing their involvement with the event (and any special interest story that may go along with it, e.g., Susie Markus is volunteering in honor of her son, who has juvenile diabetes, etc.).
- Letter from board chair to all committee volunteers.
- Letter from support group leaders (in the case of health-related causes) or letter from recipients of funds raised (e.g., a letter from children at a children's hospital), or a letter from a public official if the event benefits the community.

Day-of Volunteers

Many of the above strategies and tactics on recruiting, cultivating and recognizing committee volunteers apply to day-of volunteers as well. The basic differences are in creating a plan to recruit groups versus individual volunteers as well as individuals with a short commitment. It is a challenge not only to recruit groups, but also to retain and train these people and, most importantly, get them to show up. As a general rule, about 15% of volunteers don't show. Here's the tricky part: We tend to compensate for these no-shows by recruiting more volunteers than we need, but we do not want *too many* volunteers. Too many volunteers creates a problem in and of itself . . . bored volunteers. Bored volunteers = problems. Bored volunteers want to do something: they got up early, are typically too hot or too cold and possibly hungry; they do not want all these sacrifices to be for naught! Quite frankly, extra volunteers become a burden.

Here's a real-life example: On a two-day bike tour throughout northern Illinois and Wisconsin, we ran out of lunch. Yes, really . . . completely out. Our lunch captain was trying to get Ron's Subs in a nearby town to deliver 300 sub sandwiches in the next 20 minutes (my guess is that Ron typically sells about 75 per day), so she had a problem on her hands. In addition, a cyclist had just taken a bad fall a mile and a half away from her location. The last thing that lunch captain needed was eight too many volunteers vying to help and/or asking what they can do. You get the picture. With regards to running out of food and other war stories, make sure to read "What if? — A Guide to Plan B" in Chapter 8.

Basically, you'll want to have the most accurate guesstimate you can. To increase the volunteer show-up rate, have a solid plan in place which incorporates phone calls the week of and day before the event, volunteer mailings and incentives.

How, When and Where to Recruit Day-of Volunteers

Obviously it's a lot easier to recruit one corporation or organization (even another nonprofit) to volunteer 50 people to "work" an event for a day than it is to recruit 50 individual volunteers. Recruiting a group is 49 fewer telephone calls . . . now if that isn't an incentive, I don't know what is! As I'm sure you've discovered, if you try to recruit solely individual volunteers you will run out of time and energy. Selling a corporation on volunteering for an event is a lot easier than asking them for a donation or asking them to form a corporate team. They are often looking for "off-the-clock" (non-working hour) "team building" events. Many times, employers will give internal incentives to employees who volunteer, like a day off or a special lunch exclusively for the individuals who volunteered. Research local organizations (corps and service organizations) and put together a list of prospects. Contact the human resources (HR) departments of the companies you would like to solicit. The March of Dimes Campaign for Healthier Babies has done an excellent job of infiltrating corporate America, especially the Fortune 500s. You will often hear, "Sorry, we support the March of Dimes Walk." That's okay. *Carve out your own niche* — aim for family-owned businesses or new service organizations. Ask your HR person to join the local HR association — along with membership comes a membership list with contact names, companies, addresses and often direct telephone numbers.

Ten organizations/industries to target when recruiting:

1. Board members' corporations (ask them to assign two people, preferably a high-ranking executive and a middle manager and/or secretary).

2. Law firms (yes, really, law firms). Lawyers are often looking for good PR. Nearly all large law firms have marketing and public relations directors. Check with your local chapter of NALFMA (National Association of Law Firm Marketers).
3. Key Clubs and other service-based organizations.
4. Telephone Pioneers (the association of retired telephone operators). They are very conscientious volunteers — great for doing registration and tele-recruiting).
5. Support groups (if you are a health-related organization).
6. Motorcycle groups, such as Gold Wing Riders, a recreational motorcycle group of folks (many retired) that are amazing resources, especially for walks with routes on city streets and bicycle tours. Give 'em a telephone and they become one of the most valuable safety regulators on any event.
7. National Guard, Army and Navy (and Reserve). (They often have equipment . . . tents, etc.) These guys and gals make great route designers as well as markers.
8. Outdoorsy groups, like the Independent Order of Foresters.
9. Boy and Girl Scouts are great for clean-up (and they are required to perform service to their community in order to receive "points" to obtain coveted merit badges and pins).
10. Foreign corporations — they are always looking to be the best citizen they can be in their adopted home.

Why Corporations Need Nonprofits

- To be "good corporate citizens" in the local community and general PR
- Promotes teamwork and friendly competition between departments (companies may offer the department with the *greatest percentage of volunteers* incentives, such as a private lunch with the president, a day off or a gift certificate) and creates a working environment which isn't all work.

Recruiting for day-of volunteers should occur four to six weeks before the day of your event, giving corporations enough time to publicize it in their employee newsletters, on pay stubs and e-mail, etc.

Day-of Volunteer Training

The first rule of training your day-of volunteers is *pre-training* your day-of volunteers — training must be done prior to event day. I recommend at least one pre-event training session, held twice to accommodate the different needs of your volunteers. If your route is a logistically intricate one, I recommend meeting two times for the medical, SAG (see logistics section) and safety volunteers.

Here's the training plan:

- Training sessions to be held where you are likely to get as many people to show up as possible (one should be held in the suburbs for major cities where parking is free) at an easily identifiable meeting place. These meetings should be held on a Saturday morning as well as a weeknight in the center of your city (if that is where most business people are located).
- Training session "general session" should last no more than one and a half hours (allow for another 45 minutes or so to divide up into groups).
- Meet in schools, colleges, hotels, libraries, sponsor offices (with separate group rooms) so that specific volunteer groups (e.g., registration, lunch, finish line) can go to discuss their own responsibilities, etc., after the general session.

Recommended Agenda for Day-Of Volunteer Training Session

All volunteers must sign in on a volunteer registration form (use your brochure registration form). It is critical that they fill out *all* information: work and home telephone numbers, best time to reach them, etc. All volunteer leaders (captains) should have a complete list of his/her volunteers.

I.   Welcome and introductions of staff and walk committee members

II. Orientation

    a. Background of organization and its mission.

    b. Tie the cause to the event! If a health-related cause, ask a client, patient or family of a person affected by the disease to give a personal "testimony."

    c. Share event summary and history (if any).

    d. Give day-of procedural list or *manual** to volunteers

        1. Where they park, sign in and check out

        2. What to do in case of inclement weather (tell them to tune into your sponsor's radio station in the morning for cancellation in case of extremely bad weather)

        3. When/if they get breakfast, lunch and/or dinner breaks (this depends on the event). For walks, only lunch is served, if at all. Volunteers are always concerned with when they are to be fed. *Always* plan to deliver lunch to your volunteers.

III. Break down the group into pre-determined categories

    a. Present (with accompanying handout) volunteer responsibilities to the various groups

        1. rest-stop volunteers

        2. SAG volunteers

        3. communications volunteers

        4. registration volunteers
        (more details about these categories and specific job descriptions will be given in the next chapter.)

    b. Distribute any volunteer incentives.

This is tricky. There is always the "chicken and the egg" dilemma of "if I give them their volunteer t-shirt or hat before the event, will they show up?" *or* "will they show up because they

---

*I strongly recommend giving to each and every volunteer a training/safety manual that incorporates first aid tips, a copy of the route, and all relevant telephone numbers (key staff cell phone numbers, location of communications people and how to reach them, nearest hospitals, vendors, etc.).

have received their incentive, have taken ownership and feel more responsibility and devotion toward the event?"

    c. Question and answer period of at least 20 minutes.

    NOTE: It is preferable for each of the above categories to have its own team leader, trained prior to this general meeting. This person can be either a trusted volunteer, committee volunteer or staff member, depending on your organization size.

    Provide a second training session *for registration volunteers only.* Do not attempt to train your registration volunteers the day of the event! If your registration process does not move smoothly, you'll lose participants for the next year . . . and revenue!

    If you are in a particularly large market (or in your second or third year of your event) it may be nearly impossible to get all your volunteers together at one time. Large markets are the most likely to have multiple sites. Multiple sites equal more volunteers. In this case, I suggest breaking up your training into multiple sessions, or assigning your volunteer leaders (I prefer to always use staff, partnered with a committee member) to arrange for each individual "team."

Ways to Increase Attendance to Training:

- Send letter three weeks prior to training.
- Ask volunteer leaders/captains to personally call each volunteer (if you have multiple routes, make sure to have one volunteer leader per category per route).
- Advertise and serve food!
  Many volunteers sign up simply to meet new people. Let them know there will be time to "mingle" with other volunteers.
- Make the training fun and festive. Be sure to include their "lucky number" in the direct mail invitation to training for raffle prizes (sponsored, of course!). If possible, offer one really great prize to be raffled off. Just make sure they know the charity didn't buy the prize (volunteers hate seeing wastefulness).

For volunteers who do not show up for the training: Ask the volunteer leaders/captains to personally call them the next day and tell them you are sorry to have missed them. Ask them if they would like you to keep them on your volunteer list. If yes, send them the information and call again in one week.

Day-of Volunteer Recognition

The following are lists for different levels of recognition. The ways you recognize your volunteers will depend on the size of your organization and event. Naturally, you can mix and match these lists to meet your market and community.

- special volunteer name tags
- hat or cap
- letters to employers for personnel files
- thank you letters
- personalized note
- thank you letters from patients (if health-related cause) or board members
- invitation to post-event party
- lunch at walk
- personal call
- personal call from patient or board member
- place on walk newsletter
- list in newsletter
- subscription to year-round volunteer newsletter
- opportunity to raise money
- volunteer t-shirt
- volunteer sweatshirt (sponsored, if possible)
- recognition at walk party

Tangible "incentives" are not enough, however; most volunteers need to feel and hear they are appreciated, often publicly. The same way we try to identify sponsors' needs, we must also identify volunteers' needs. Why are they participating? Most of us do not need to be reminded to do this — it's our business. But it's a good idea to remind your staff to generously thank the volunteers before, during and after.

Eight
Logistics

Five tips from pros who learned about logistics the hard way:

• Don't let logistics drive recruitment.
• If it ain't broke, don't fix it.
• Don't sweat the small stuff.
• Keep your eye on the donut, not on the hole.
  (Don't get caught up in minor details . . . always be able to see the BIG picture.)
• Don't reinvent the wheel ("borrow" ideas and *enhance*).

Route Identification and Design

If you've produced sporting events before, you know how important the route is. Whether a walk, bike tour or run, the event should be unique and have *something for everyone*, especially for

Location, Location, Location
(six no-fail walk routes):

- Park district bicycle paths
- Golf courses (which have been closed for the day)
- Historic or quaint neighborhoods or towns
- A zoo
- Botanical gardens
- Near a lake, river or stream (or ocean!)

families and the physically challenged. Below are key route considerations.

The route should:

- Not impede emergency, fire, police or paramedic vehicles.
- Have varied levels of challenge.
- Be conveniently located (within 5 to 25 miles from participants).
- Incorporate a shorter-distance option for physically challenged participants and families — but *never* an entirely separate route.
- Not conflict with public transportation, such as buses, trolleys and trains.
- Not interfere with people trying to reach hospitals, the airport, their own residences, businesses, places of worship and public facilities.
- Have enough parking spaces for at least 65% of your participants, depending on how close your route is from participants' homes. Most participants will drive with a friend or two. Watch out for "parking" that is on grass or, worse yet, on dirt. If it rains the night before, you may be in *big* trouble. People who can't park don't stay.
- Have paved roads, preferably walking paths (except, of course, in the case of long-distance bike tours).
- Have at least one large, covered area — and preferably an indoor area — for registration.

- Have police assistance at major intersections.
- Have enough room for emergency vehicles to get to the route in the case of any injury.
- Allow space for your supply truck to clear nearby road overpasses.
- Be near hospitals.
- Be between 8 and 12 miles long.

Identifying Route Hazards

I don't need to tell you the route must be safe. It's surprising how many times problems could have been prevented if someone (it's the event manager's responsibility) did a trial run of the route before event day. Don't assume anything! Here's a checklist of important risk considerations:

✓ Check with the streets and sanitation department in your municipality for upcoming road work.

(I once had to transport 40+ cyclists from a rural town in southern Illinois because a remote farm road had just been tarred. More than 40 cyclists rode through the hot tar before we knew about it! It wasn't pretty — and it was costly as we felt we had a responsibility to the participants (we picked up the cost of new tires).

✓ Walk your proposed route (or drive in the case of a long-distance bike tour).

Check out the level of challenge, pace and placement of rest stops, medical and safety support and dangerous intersections.

✓ Meet with local police before planning the route!

I can't stress this point enough! Police departments are invaluable resources! They know their areas and can often map out an entire route right before your eyes. Don't re-invent the wheel — they know the hazards!

Never chance questionable neighborhoods!

Making Your Route Accessible

This is a touchy subject. I personally believe ALL routes should be fully accessible, despite the costs. Why? Because not only is ensuring accessibility the right thing to do, it helps increase awareness of the challenges physically handicapped individuals go through. It also helps garner support through the media. But most of all, it helps recruit physically handicapped participants! Regardless of whether or not your organization is health-related, your route should be accessible, despite the added costs of special equipment.

Seven Questions to Ask About Route Accessibility:

- Does the path allow for the width of a wheelchair (minimum width of path should be at least three feet)?
- Are there any gravel areas?
- Are there any steps?
- Do we have at least one handicapped-accessible toilet at every rest stop and start/finish location?
- Are all doorways (in the case of inside registration) accessible?

Distance

Distance is a funny thing. Some people believe more is better. Others prefer quality. Try to incorporate both through multiple route options if your budget (and staff and volunteer commitments) warrants. Remember, the longer the route, the more rest stops, the more stops, the more food, toilet facilities, the greater cost (or sponsorships). Here are my recommended distances for walking, one-day biking events and long-distance bike tours (and remember, these are non-competitive events):

- Walks   From 8 to 12 miles
- One-day cycling events   From 50 to 100 miles
- Two-day cycling events   From 100 to 150 miles

Miles or Kilometers?

This is strictly a personal choice. Check other events around town. My personal view is that it doesn't make a difference, except in running races where kilometers are clearly preferred. However, there is the "$20,000 question": *Will we raise more money if the distance is in kilometers because there are more kilometers per mile?* Most of the participants' sponsors donate a flat amount, not per mile or kilometer.

Marking Your Route

What is a route **marking?** It is a sign or symbol along the route that identifies the path. Markings can also be motivational, but the primary purpose is guidance. For walks, you'll need two or four dedicated and trustworthy volunteers, preferably from the volunteer committee, to mark the route. For long-distance bicycle tours, you'll need two or three volunteers to mark the route up to the turn-around point and another two or three volunteers to mark the ride back to the start. It is imperative that the volunteers and/or staff who helped design the route be active participants in marking the route.

Route markings are a must. *Don't assume anything except that your participants don't know the route* (regardless of the detail in the route maps you provide for them). Assume participants can't read, because they don't. (Sorry, but they don't.) It's our responsibility to take them by the hand and feed them crumbs along the way; they do not know the route like you do, especially if your route is on streets. Again, with cycling events it is particularly important to mark carefully and often. One wrong turn and the cyclist may ride onto a heavily traveled road.

Where do we mark our route?

- Mark your route every 1/4 mile for walks and 1/2 miles for bicycle tours and always before a rest stop.
- At all crossings, major points, hazards and *turns*!
- Preferably eye level, but do not staple to trees!
- On the side of the route — never, never in the middle of a path.

- On the path, using spray chalk (never paint!). Spray chalk can be purchased at almost any hardware store.

What do we use to mark the path?

- Strong, plastic-covered signs stapled to wooden stakes work best, but be sure to have a rubber mallet to pound the stakes into the ground! (And always test your signs first to make sure they will stay up!)
- Volunteers with bull horns for especially hazardous crossings.
- Again, use spray chalk to "write" motivational messages directly on the walking path. Never use paint.

When do we mark the route?

The best time to mark the route is the day before the event, beginning at dusk for a walk and very early morning the day before for a bicycle tour. Do not mark a walk route *during* the day or the signs will be pulled up or blown down before your event begins. (If there is rain or high winds in the forecast, then marking the walk route the morning of the event is the only option left. If your walkers are scheduled to start walking around 9:00 a.m., then the marking of the route should begin around 5:00 a.m.) Spreading volunteers out in sections is best, but not necessary. Some volunteers prefer to mark the entire route themselves for continuity. For a cycling event, it is critical to mark during the day as it can be a 10-hour project.

The event manager should never mark the route her- or himself. Route managers must always be managing and delegating, not physically working. They should never lift a box or they will get caught up micro-managing the event. Remember, keep your eye on the donut, not the hole!

Participant Route Map

A route map should be given out to each participant. Even if your route is basic, maps can be motivational, informative, educational (about the cause) and, best of all, it gives you one more opportunity to thank your sponsors by including their logos. Here are some questions your walkers will be asking themselves: How far is the next port-a-pottie? I'm tired. Should I take this passing SAG van now or can I make it to the next rest stop — how much farther? Will there be food at the next rest stop? Your route map should answer these questions. Note that it should be simple, yet fun and informative.

Permits

Your event can make a significant impact on not only your nonprofit, but on your community as well. It can foster a sense of community for a city, town or village . . . even a neighborhood. It can even add to the quality of life. On the other hand, your event could negatively impact your nonprofit's reputation, your sponsors and the general community if it is not planned safely. Obtaining permits is not done to cause your organization grief. It is done to protect your organization and the general public.

Just because you have identified your dream route, printed 25,000 brochures and have announced that your event is taking place on a certain date or time does not mean you have the legal right to that route! Planner beware! I can't tell you the number of conflicts I have come across because either I or another event planner inadvertently forgot to secure the route and date with the permit office (most often through the park district or city). The permit process can be frightening, but it doesn't have to be. Occasionally, permit administrators are demanding; it's their job to protect the public. Be sensitive to this and dot your i's and cross your t's on all permit applications (see Exhibit 8.1, the special events permit application). The City of Chicago, which produces the single largest special event in the country, The Taste of Chicago, as well as hundreds of neighborhood festivals, sporting events and other events, has a strict permit application process for all special events. They have one of the best (and most efficient) permit application processes in the country. Take a look before you begin planning your route — the application is packed with questions that will make you really think about your route.

And remember, a carefully thought out risk management plan (later in this chapter) will not only give the permit office the

---

SPECIAL EVENTS PERMIT APPLICATION

I. **TITLE, PURPOSE AND BRIEF DESCRIPTION OF EVENT:**

_____   □ New Application

_____   □ Renewal or Change in
                                                Application

_____

Refer media or citizen inquiries to: _____

        Telephone_____ or_____

II. **APPLICANT AUTHORIZATION**

Attach a written communication from the organization in whose name the event will be
advertised which authorizes you the applicant, to apply for this special events permit on its or
their behalf.

Applicant's Name: _____ Title: _____

Address:_____

Mailing Address: _____

Affiliation: _____

Daytime Phone: _____ Evening Phone: _____ Emergency Phone: _____

III. **EVENT PRINCIPALS:**

On the next sheet, please list names, addresses, and telephone numbers of all principals
involved in any way in the proposed special event. Include professional event organizers, event
promoters, financial underwriters, commercial sponsors, charitable agencies for whose benefit
the event is being produced, the organization or organizations in whose name the event is being
advertised, and all other administratively, financially, and organizationally involved as principals
in the production of the proposed special event. Make additional copies of the next sheet as
needed to include all of the principals involved in the proposed special event.

Page 1 of 10

(Exhibit 8.1) Here are a few pages from Chicago's special events permit application. Filling it out can be a daunting task, but not doing it or leaving it until the last minute can cause even more problems.

Reprinted with permission from the City of Chicago.

information they need to process your application, it will help your organization get insurance and produce a safe event.

There are many types of permits, and each city has its own way of issuance. For most cities, however, the following process is fairly standardized:

   1. Contact the park district where you would like to hold the event.

Name: _____

Organization/Business/Agency/Affiliation:_____

Mailing Address: _____

Affiliation: _____

Daytime Phone: _____ Evening Phone: _____ Emergency Phone: _____

Title and Functional Responsibility with Regard to the Event: _____

_____

_____

_____

Will this person have authority to cancel or greatly modify event plans?

☐ Yes   ☐ No

Will this person be present at the event area or areas and in charge of the event at all times?

☐ Yes   ☐ No

Name: _____

Organization/Business/Agency/Affiliation:_____

Mailing Address: _____

Affiliation: _____

Daytime Phone: _____ Evening Phone: _____ Emergency Phone: _____

Title and Functional Responsibility with Regard to the Event: _____

_____

_____

_____

Will this person have authority to cancel or greatly modify event plans?

☐ Yes   ☐ No

Will this person be present at the event area or areas and in charge of the event at all times?

☐ Yes   ☐ No   Page 2 of 10

(In the case of long-distance cycling events you may have to obtain permits in every city or town you plan to ride through.) They will send you a formal application that tells you their fees. Most districts ask you to contact them at least 60 days in advance. *I recommend one full year.* This, of course, is not always possible. But if you know your date, make sure you are in line on January 2, when most parks issue their permits — you don't want to lose a route because a family picnic got in the way. Which reminds me: Often, *separate permits must be obtained for pavilions.* Just because you have secured a route with a permit, doesn't mean you

IV.   **REQUESTED EVENT COMPONENTS:**

A.   Requested day and date (first choice): _____

B.   Alternate days and dates:

  _____

  _____

  _____

C.   Requested hours of operation, from _____ AM/PM to _____ AM/PM

D.   Set up beginning day and date _____, Time_____ AM/PM

  Dismantle by day and date _____, Time_____ AM/PM

E.   Describe the number and type of animals to be used in the event: _____

F.   Attach a draft of the entry form for participants/spectators.

G.   Anticipated number of participants: _____ and spectators: _____

V.   **INSURANCE:**

Attach to this application either an insurance policy or a certificate of insurance including the policy number, amount and the provision that the City is included as an additional insured. (Please note that insurance requirements depend upon the risk level of the event. Also, if your event can be classified as a first Amendment expressive activity, insurance requirements can be waived under certain circumstances.)

VI.   **SANITATION:**

Attach your "Plan for Cleanup/Material Preservation". Include the number, type and location of trash containers to be provided for the event. Indicate who and how many will be responsible for emptying and cleaning up around containers *during* the event. Indicate who and how many will be responsible for cleaning up after animals if they are to be used in the event. Indicate who and how many will be responsible for cleaning up the event area *after* the event. Describe the number, type and location of portable toilets to be provided for the event (or permanent toilets to be used for the event). Include any other plan you have for ensuring post-event cleanliness and material preservation of city facilities, equipment, premises and streets.

Page 3 of 10

have the pavilions along the route! Check with your park district or issuing party.

> 2. Complete application and all necessary support documents (route maps, etc.).
> 3. Send fee (application fees, user fees and security deposits are all standard with most park districts).

Many times nonprofits are charged 50% of fees based on their 501(c) 3 status. Regardless, 30 days before an event, the user (you) must provide the following:

- $X amount user fee
- $X amount security deposit
- $1–2 million certificate of insurance (more on this later in this chapter under Risk Management)

Here's a sure-fire, step-by-step checklist for getting a permit issued *fast* (the permit coordinator will be so overwhelmed if you have the following information in advance, you will fly though the red tape):

1. **Be prepared — know your route.** Have your route drawn, to scale, marking the following: number and placement of toilet facilities; number and placement of police or traffic controllers; number and locations of first aid stations; internal security and crowd control plans; nighttime lighting (if any); and any other requirement to protect the health and safety of the participants and the public.
2. **Have a clean-up plan** (volunteers should be assigned in advance).
3. **Are alcoholic beverages being served?** If so, you'll need a special permit, not to mention additional ("dram shop") insurance (we'll discuss this in greater detail under Event Insurance/Risk Management).
4. **Will you have music, sound amplification or any other noise impact? What about a generator?** If so, you may need a special permit.

There are many, many other permit considerations, including fire department requirements, insurance requirements, food service considerations, concessions and many more. Get a copy of your proposed site(s) permit application(s).

Equipment

Equipment, arguably, is the highest expense in your event budget. If you can get equipment donated, great. It has been my experience, however, that it is not worth the time spent, except in the case of trucking. There are many trucking companies out there that are willing to donate their time and a truck, especially on Sundays when they aren't delivering. Talk to companies that do local routes, not national ones (companies doing national runs cannot predict if a truck will get lost, break down, etc., leaving a big window of opportunity for disaster). The local trucking company should be a large one with lots of warehouse space (called a terminal), so you can also store sponsors' products. Often, trucking sponsors will also pick up donated items on their routes. As far as sponsored toilets (port-a-potties), I have only seen sponsored ones once — and it was pretty damn funny! However, most sponsors do not want their company/product associated with a toilet, let alone a port-a-pottie! So, again, don't waste precious time. Concentrate on logistics, not sponsorship.

There is a lot to cover. First, let's start with basic needs as well as some alternatives. Obviously, if you can hold your event (at least registration and lunch) under a pavilion, the cost goes down. If you are unable to secure an indoor location(s) for your site(s), I recommend always providing tents for the key areas (start/finish, registration, lunch, and at the rest stops, at least covering the volunteers). Often this is not possible. Yes, they are expensive, but if it rains, not only will valuable information be saved (walker IDs, pledge sheets, etc.), but the walkers will be appreciative of having lunch under a roof. Or worse yet, when it rains, people leave — never to return. Let's not forget the most important reason for having a secure registration area: security. Hopefully you'll have lots of pledge money coming in — you don't want strangers having access. Here is a list of must-have equipment:

• **Other tents:** Tents are not required, but they can take a mom-and-pop event to the next level or help separate your event from your competitor. Most park district cycling path routes have pavilions which are just as good as tents, but at no expense. Take these opportunities when they present themselves or plan your walk route only along paths that have these accommodations. But, if your community doesn't have this opportunity, tents are always a good idea for the registration/lunch and t-shirt giveaway areas. *Recommendation:* Always combine the registration tent with the lunch tent. Once walkers have left the start, set up the registration area for lunch. For tent sizes, always consult your vendor; he or she will know best. For registration, set up 6' or 8' tables end-to-end along the perimeter of the tent. This will keep walkers from entering the tent.

• **Port-a-potties:** (also called port-a-johns and port-a-lets, depending on which brand you use. Again, obviously, it's better to have your rest stops located where facilities are already provided. However, this is often not possible. Port-a-potties are about $50 apiece, depending on where you're located and what company you use. I like Waste Management. They are always on time, have clean facilities, and know their way around in the dark. *Recommendation:* Five port-a-potties per 1,000 walkers plus one handicapped-accessible port-a-pottie per 1,000. Deliver late the night before an event or early the morning of. I prefer the night before in the case of misplacement. But if you are holding your walk near a lake or river and people hang out there, don't expect your toilets to be in good condition in the morning!

• **Sink:** Yes, you'll need a portable sink. Again, through a waste management company. Even if you sneak by without one for the participants (which, by the way, they ask for), you may be zapped by the health department for code violations if you're serving food.

• **Trash dumpster:** Many cities, towns and villages will require you to provide your own dumpster for trash as part of the permit process. No provision for trash, no permit.

• **Vehicles:** The following vehicles are a must for nearly any sporting event. If you have a strong volunteer base and are doing a relatively small walk (less than 200 people), trucks may be avoided. Either way, be wary of insurance risks (risk management will be discussed shortly).

1. **Refrigerated truck** (if needed): One 18' truck per 1,000 walkers.

2. **SAG vehicles:** SAGS are used for safety as well as to pick up weary participants. (SAGS can be personal cars, preferably station wagons or vans, but are often larger (buses), depending on the type of event, route and size of event. A few years back we had Mercedes-Benz as SAG vehicles! They picked up weary participants from each stop. In the case of bike tours, this is obviously not possible. (For bike tours, SAGS must be *at least* a mini

pick-up truck. And, remember, for bicycle tours especially, the truck must be able to hold not only the passengers, but their bikes as well.) *Recommendation:* Five vans per 1,000 walkers or two school buses per 1,000 walkers. Vans are preferred because of their maneuverability and access. Don't forget a handicapped-accessible van if your route is publicized as being so. Where vans are prohibited, use mopeds and/or cyclists to monitor walking routes (preferably first-aid trained and armed with a cell phone or radio).

3. **Supply trucks** (Important note: Load truck backwards! First on is last off!): We once loaded a truck as we read stop 1, stop 2, stop 3. On event day at 5 a.m. as our volunteers were unloading, they had to remove everything at the first stop to get to the back where the first rest stop's supplies were! Supply trucks can be vans, station wagons, etc. It is imperative, however, to make sure you will have enough room before you go to load your trucks, cars and/or vans! Dry runs are almost never done, but always call a terminal manager of a trucking company to find out how much can fit in each truck.

4. **Generators:** If there is no access to electricity, you'll need a generator. Check with your equipment vendor. Make sure he/she carries the top-of-the-line generators. My experience is that the extra money is worth it. Generators are the most volatile equipment you can rent. *Recommendation:* The Honda brand generator is the most quiet and most dependable. Be sure to have a few extension cords on hand.

Selecting and Negotiating with Vendors

Choosing an equipment vendor is tough. You must continually weigh cost versus benefits. Typically, a full-service vendor will be higher, but the peace of mind may be worth it. But what if you just can't afford a top-of-the-line vendor? (Most of us can't — and you'll rarely see a rental company donating the type and amount of equipment sporting events need. The best you can hope for is to have a corporation sponsor a tent.) List your priorities, then rank them. (*Always rank toilet facilities #1!* The lack of toilet facilities is — consistently — right up there with running out of food. People won't come back if this happens. And as we will discuss shortly in Chapter 11, past participants are the best future participants because they cost less to recruit and they raise more money. So keep them happy!)

Next, take a look at your organization's event calendar. Include all events, donor- and pledge-based. Group your next year's needs together and ask yourself the following questions: How many times did we order a generator? How many times did we get that great big 40′ x 40′ tent? Naturally, if you consolidate your equipment needs and offer one vendor all your business for the year, you'll have a lot more bargaining power. This is easier said than done. For us mere mortals, we're lucky enough to get bids in 24 hours before event day! Therefore, I suggest going to the smaller guy, the family-run vendor in the neighborhood. Usually he/she has less overhead and — except in the case of large-scale events — will have the supply at a much lower price. (Even the large equipment suppliers don't have all the equipment all the time. Often, they borrow from one another.) Regardless of which vendor you choose, you must stay on top of things in terms of delivery time and placement.

Here are a few tips when dealing with equipment vendors:

- Negotiate hard.
- Always give them detailed site maps with diagrams with the words "no later than ____ a.m." Did I mention *detailed?*
- Always provide *written* directions from their location as well as a map.

Signs

I remember the first time I received a sponsor banner. I was so excited, I thought I'd made the big-time. It seems rather silly now, but I think it is still important to feel that way when you see a new sign. Signage is much more than sponsor banners. It is recognition, it is a way to direct and a way to control. Signs are extremely important for safety. Without proper signage, an event can be ruined, both financially and logistically.

I explained in detail how to mark a route, but in this section I am going to speak to the importance of and give promotional tips on signage/banners in the following areas: start/finish, registration and sponsorship.

Start/Finish Banner: The start/finish banner is more than simply a start/finish banner. It is an opportunity. Yes, an opportunity to acknowledge sponsors/sell sponsorships as well as to educate participants on the cause. When I see a start/finish banner that doesn't incorporate the mission or doesn't showcase the main sponsors' logos, I see missed opportunities. Be sure to incorporate the start/finish banner opportunities in all cash (or significant in-kind) sponsorship proposals. One more word about start/finish signage: image. The start/finish banner is the largest banner you'll have at your event. It is extremely important that this banner be professionally done. No cardboard sign here. If you must use handmade signs, use them in other areas of the event or on smaller routes if you have multi-site walks. But for your largest or only route (I call it the promotional route), professionally designed and produced signs are *mandatory.* Remember, we're not "mom and pop" anymore. If it's not in your budget, it should be. It conveys not only the image of the event, but the image of your cause and its mission to the participants and to the general public as well (especially if your route is visible from the street or if there are media present). A lot rides (literally) on that sign.

Registration Signs: Good registration signage is important. Here it is not quite as important to be pretty (although they must be uniform). It must, however, be *visible.* The single biggest mistake people make when using registration signage is that they tape or staple the signs to the front of registration tables. *Wrong.* (Again, I learned this the hard way when 4,000 people couldn't tell the difference between pre-registration and day-of-registration tables. (Of course, the people who had pre-registered were angered when they had to stand in lines the same as day-of registrants.) Why? Because the signs aren't visible once one person is standing in front of them. ALL REGISTRATION SIGNS MUST BE ABOVE EYE LEVEL! *(Don't forget your ladder on the day of an event . . . really!)*

When I use the term "registration" I mean the entire registration process. Therefore, you should be prepared to have the following signs on hand (as well as a thick black marker and BIG white poster board):

- Team Registration
- Pre-Registration
- Day-of Registration (otherwise known as "Walk-ons")
- Team Photos
- Team Meeting Place
- "Heart & Sole" Club Registration (for past participants only)
- Golden Feet Registration (for people who raised over $250 the previous year. Inform them of this special privilege through personalized direct mail. See Chapter 6, Communications Development.)

   (These "club" names were designed to help boost recruitment. These special clubs are actually low-cost incentives. More on recruitment strategies in Chapter 11.)
- XYZ Walk Parking (and, always, special parking areas for the handicapped participants and for the top of the top fund raisers ($500 and up).

Sponsor Signs: Probably what we all think about when we think of signage and banners. Sponsor banners are *vital* for these reasons:

1. They give the sponsor recognition.
2. Sponsor banners "validate" the event.

Participants commonly think to themselves, "If XYZ company is sponsoring this walk, it must be a good cause [good walk, good whatever]."

These two reasons are why it is so important to place these banners in their proper places. Yes, proper. Often we include where the banner is going to be placed in our sponsorship proposal. If the sponsor is in attendance and the banner is not where we say it will be, the sponsor may not be pleased. Banners should always be given to one designated (and trusted) volunteer or staff person who *will be at the event on time* (if you have the luxury).

It is also important to have a specific diagram *only* for banner placement. It really is that important. And many times when we get into the rush of the event and the minutiae of details, we forget the most important ones. Sponsor banners are those important details.

The Safety Plan — Identifying, Evaluating and Reducing Risk

Undertaking a special event, particularly a sporting event, raises the possibility of loss of property, damage to property, loss of income through liability to others, and of life and even death. Accidents happen. People forget, don't finish things, are tired, overlook safety precautions "just this once," and sometimes just don't care. Nonprofit events are not exempt from people acting negligently, foolishly — even criminally. We must do everything within our power — and more — to ensure not only an enjoyable event, but a safe one.

Caroline Cogtella, risk manager for the City of Chicago, stated the following on event risk:

> Every nonprofit event has its risks. Whether a church bingo party, a charity ball or a sporting event, you must identify your exposures, look at alternatives to reducing that risk and decide on the best ones. Then, you must evaluate the effectiveness of the plan. In order to analyze the risk, you must look at many different areas, including:
>
> 1. Your route.
> 2. The age of participants.
> 3. What are the safety procedures you are going to implement in the case of an emergency?
> 4. What is your worker's comp exposure?
>
> These and many other factors are all critical areas in event risk management and in obtaining liability coverage for your event and participants.

Risk management must be integrated into your event at each level. Risk management is the process of making and carrying out decisions that minimize adverse effects of potential losses of an event. Effective risk management should incorporate ways in which, if the event is conducted in the absolute safest manner and if something does go wrong, the loss does not further impact the organization. The responsibility of risk management should not fall on one person alone — it is a shared responsibility — from volunteers to the executive director of your organization.

Goals of Risk Management

1. To prevent event cancellation
2. To grow gradually
3. To reduce anxiety about risk
4. To operate within the city, town or village laws
5. To fulfill social responsibilities (to participant, public, etc.)
6. To fund raise

The Risk Management Process

1. Risk Analysis
   What could cause a loss?
   What is exposed to a loss?
   Who would suffer the loss?
   What are the financial consequences?
   What are the ethical consequences?

2. Examine Risk Management Tactics
   Risk control
   Risk financing

3. Planning Effective Actions or Techniques
   (More on this later when we discuss "Plan B")

4. Implementing Risk Management Recommendations

5. Post-event: Evaluating, Monitoring and Enhancing the Program

Why Losses Occur

- *Harried or inadequate planning.*
- *Inadequate management.*
- *Human error.*
- *Unsafe/uncontrollable physical conditions* (weather, cleanliness, overcrowding, exposure to elements or hazardous materials).
- *Uncontrollable energy* (anger, frustration, excitement, etc.).
- *The domino effect.* One thing affects another. A failure triggers yet another failure, e.g., there is a thunderstorm and people can no longer walk along the path. You send in a bus and, because of the rain, too many people rush onto the bus. The bus driver can't see out his window because too many people are blocking his view, so he gets into an accident.
- *Poor communications.* Because of the nature of nonprofit events, most take place only once a year. Therefore, many people have never worked with each other. Good communication (discussed shortly) is critical.

The following two approaches can greatly reduce risk:

1. Eliminate risk — cancel the event if the risk is too great, or eliminate the cause of the problem.
2. Legally transfer the risk to someone else — contract others to perform a risky task, then they are responsible for liabilities in that area (ask for certificate of insurance).

Top Risk Factors

1. Risk factors should be identified before the event, not after a crisis.
2. Risk factors should identified while there is still time to take precautions.
3. Risks are as likely to occur when setting up or tearing down an event as during the event.

4. Risk factors are real even when everything turns out OK. "Luck happens!"
5. Hire a professional risk manager (better yet, network with board members and ask who they use for their company).

Security Planning

A security plan should address all key risk factors identified. Do not "adapt" a walk security plan to fit the needs of a bike tour. Every event is unique and never exactly the same. Have a written security plan that is handed out to all key volunteers. Anything not in writing can be construed later as not existing. Here's a basic, yet comprehensive security outline:

I. Preliminary Security Measures
   a. Map of event/vicinity
   b. Diagram of venue (site)

II. Security Personnel
   a. Who (private, police, volunteers, etc.)
   b. Chain of command
   c. Coordination/communication between

III. Schedule and Timeline
   a. Planning sessions
   b. Training classes
   c. Pre-event "briefing" sessions
   d. Sign in/out of equipment
   e. Parking
   f. Start/finish
   g. Route
   h. Registration/crowd control & guidance
   i. VIP protection
   j. Opening/closing of food stations
   k. Alcoholic beverage distribution. (Only recommended at the end of a bike tour. Walks are too family oriented.)
   l. End of event and clean-up

IV. Assignments
   a. Command post (or command center)
   b. Traffic control
   c. Parking lots
   d. Specially designated areas (VIP, delivery, handicapped, staff, volunteers, etc.)
   e. Registration (cash collection security)
   f. First aid stations

V. Equipment
   a. Signage
   b. Communication equipment
   c. Vehicles (cars, trucks, golf carts, etc.)
   d. Incentives (t-shirts, hats, water bottles, etc.)
   e. Other (extension cords, tape, clipboards, etc.)

VI. Emergency Procedures
   a. Incident report
   b. Witness report
   c. Crisis management plan (for tornadoes, heat, etc.)
   d. Security response to injuries
   e. Media/public relations guidelines

Insurance

The above lists on risk management can make anyone's head spin. But as you can clearly see, risk management is an integral part of any event's success. And, *insurance is required 99% of the time to obtain a permit.* So, it's not only a luxury . . . *it's a necessity.*

Insurance is (or should be) a budgeted expense — simply, it's a cost of doing business. If your organization is independent and you do not have access to a planned national insurance program, you must do the investigating on your own. However, I strongly recommend seeking a risk management consultant to do the legwork. He or she will save you money in the long run, often negotiating costs. Risk managers cannot issue insurance, but they can help determine what your risks are, your insurance needs and where to find insurance (many insurance brokers have never done a "special event." A risk management consultant can help locate an insurance provider that has had experience doing similar events.

Celeste Watts, president of Risk Management and Information Systems, Inc., and former risk manager for the Chicago Park District, offers this advice on cost-cutting insurance tips for non-profit events:

- Check with your city permit office for master insurance programs for special groups (nonprofits, wedding parties, corporate picnics, etc.). Park districts and other permit issuing departments will require a "certificate of insurance" (written proof of insurance issued to the park district for a certain amount, usually one million dollars). In some cases, these issuing organizations will make the certificate of insurance affordable through a "group plan," grouping other nonprofits and individuals booking the same facility and location throughout the year.
- Purchase the insurance on your own, negotiating the brokers' commissions. Discounts are not given in the insurance industry. However, a broker can reduce or donate his/her commission and/or fee to the charity. The standard broker's commission is 10% to 15% of the policy. Ask the broker to reduce his commission, or ask him/her to offer a set fee in place of the commission.

Again, I strongly recommend hiring a qualified risk manager like Celeste to investigate your risk needs. The cost will be returned tenfold through their ability to identify your risks and help eliminate them, through negotiating insurance commissions and through matching you with a broker who knows what your organization does.

Regardless of whether your organization is national in scope or a one-person show, you'll need good liability insurance, covering both employees and volunteers (named insured). Staff, volunteers and participants are usually covered under a comprehensive general liability policy for any bodily injury or property damage they may cause to a third party. Personal coverage usually falls under your organization's worker's compensation insurance and often only covers them for an injury sustained during and connected with the event. Here are a few other event insurance questions you should ask:

1. Are rental vehicles covered?
2. Are staff/volunteers driving these vehicles covered?
3. Do we have physical damage insurance (comprehensive fire, theft, and collision) on donated vehicles?

Waivers must be signed by all volunteers (see Exhibit 8.6 for a sample of waiver, but always have an attorney and an insurance carrier review any waiver). Always put participant waivers on *all* registration forms.

Insurance can even be purchased to guarantee your event financially, in the case of a disaster. But be wary: the cost is almost always prohibitive.

When Accidents Happen

Naturally, all incidents or accidents — from a scrape on a pinkie finger to a stroke — should be handled in accordance with safety procedures outlined in your safety manual. Once the injured person(s) has been taken care of, you *must* complete incident/accident and witness forms (see Exhibit 8.2 for sample forms). These forms should be filled out by the medical team leader, if possible, and at least two non-related witnesses, if possible.

All route volunteers (from SAG drivers to rest stop volunteers) should be given several copies of incident/accident and witness forms in their "Volunteer Booklet," along with the following numbers:

- 911
- Police
- Fire
- Closest hospital to each stop (and directions for family)
- Cell numbers of all medical volunteers (or access to radio or ham communications)

incident investigation report

general information

area of incident_____

executive director notified   YES (____)   NO (____)

walk coordinator's name_____

walk attendance_____ time of incident_____ a.m./p.m.

number of people involved in incident_____

weather conditions   _____ clear   _____ rain

                            _____ cloudy   _____ temperature

light level   _____ daylight _____ dark   _____ dusk   _____ dawn

classification   _____ road related   _____ walker caused

                            _____ non-road related   _____ walker caused

                            _____serious injury/illness   _____illness

                            _____minor injury/illness   _____non-injury   _____motor vehicle related

                            other_____

location:

____starting line   ____lunch area

____registration   ____finish line

____rest stop, 1st

____rest stop, 2nd   closest street_____

type of incident

____fall   ____over-exertion

____motor vehicle   ____collision non-motor vehicle

____bodily action   ____animal/insect bite/sting

____road hazard   ____other

incident information

injured party name(s)   _____

                         _____

witness name(s)   _____

                         _____

related party name(s)   _____

                         _____

(Exhibit 8.2) To protect your volunteers and your organization, make sure that incident/accident and witness forms are filled out whenever anyone is hurt, no matter how minor the injury seems. This way, you can prove that you took the best action to help the injured person.

describe exact location of incident

_____

_____

_____

scene coordinator's analysis _____

_____

describe any immediate action taken _____

_____

additional comments regarding incident _____

_____

names of staff/volunteers working or responding to incident:

1. _____ 4. _____
2. _____ 5. _____
3. _____ 6. _____

| witness statements taken? | (___) **YES** | (___) **NO** |
| statements attached | (___) **YES** | (___) **NO** |

| volunteer statements taken? | (___) **YES** | (___) **NO** |
| statements attached | (___) **YES** | (___) **NO** |

photographs taken?   (___) **YES** (___) **NO**

date taken   ____ / ____ / ____

taken by:_____

walk coordinator's signature:_____

date_____

Safety Teams

The following teams should be recruited six weeks before an event to ensure a safe walking event:

Medical Teams

    a. Nurses

    b. Paramedics (EMTs, PTs)

```
 _____

                                           report # _____
   date incident occurred _____ time _____       rider # _____
   date incident reported _____ time _____       walker # _____

   personal information
   name (last)_____ (first)_____ (m.i.) ____
   s.s.n. _____ age _____ sex: M   F
   address_____
   phone (      ) _____

   incident information
   description of what occurred _____
   _____
   _____
   _____
   location _____

   nature of injury/illness
   ____ 1. amputation          ____ 6. contusion          ____ 11. allergy       ____ 16. heat
   ____ 2. abrasion/friction burn ____ 7. fracture confirmed ____ 12. tooth injury  ____ 17. sting bite
   ____ 3. laceration/puncture  ____ 8. dislocation        ____ 13. cold injury    ____ 18. personal illness
   ____ 4. chemical burn        ____ 9. foreign body       ____ 14. electrical shock ____ 19. pain unknown
   ____ 5. thermal burn         ____ 10. sprain, strain    ____ 15. bleeding       ____ 20. other

   part of body
   ____ 1. eye  L  R            ____ 6. shoulder  L  R     ____ 11. finger          ____ 16. ankle  L  R
   ____ 2. head                 ____ 7. arm  L  R          ____ 12. trunk int. organ ____ 17. foot  L  R
   ____ 3. face                 ____ 8. dislocation        ____ 13. hip  L  R        ____ 18. toe
   ____ 4. neck                 ____ 9. wrist  L  R        ____ 14. leg  L  R        ____ 19. nose
   ____ 5. back                 ____ 10. hand  L  R        ____ 15. knee  L  R       ____ 20. ear  L  R
                                                                                     ____ 21. tooth
                                                                                     ____ 22. internal
                                                                                     ____ 23. other

   first aid treatment given
   ____ 1. none adminstrd   ____ 9. foreign body removal  ____ 17. antacid
   ____ 2. examined         ____ 10. cold application     ____ 18. sting kill
   ____ 3. cleansed         ____ 11. rest & cool warm     ____ 19. anti-diarrhea
   ____ 4. bandaged         ____ 12. oxygen               ____ 20. anti-nausea
   ____ 5. wrapped          ____ 13. C.P.R.               ____ 21. antihistamine
   ____ 6. splinted         ____ 14. aspirin              ____ 22. other
   ____ 7. glutose          ____ 15. non-aspirin          _____
   ____ 8. eye rinse        ____ 16. antiseptic ointment  _____
   description of treatment rendered:_____
   _____
```

vital signs

time	pulse	b.p.	temp
1			
2			
3			
4			

```
   individual is: allergic to_____ currently under Rx_____
   surgical medical history_____
   disposition
   rescue squad dispatched? YES____ NO____   paramedic unit dispatched? YES____ NO____
   ambulance____ medical vehicle____ other____ time arrived at hospital_____
   vehicle attendants_____
   ...........................................................................
   medical scene coordinator signature_____ date_____
```

first aid incident report

   c. Doctors
   d. Residents at local hospitals
   e. Podiatrists (you'll need them!)

Medical teams of two should be stationed at the start/finish and at every rest stop. Mobile medical teams (cyclists) are encouraged, but sometimes present more of a hazard, depending on the number of walkers and the width of the path. If it's summer time, have a canopy and lawn chairs at every medical site for treatment.

SAG Support

a. Buses
b. Vans
c. Cars/station wagons

You'll need several SAG vehicles on your route. Again, SAG vehicles are used strictly to pick up weary participants. Most walking routes are 9 to 12 miles and are a challenge for even the fittest. Before you select the type of SAG vehicle(s) to use, inspect your route and determine which vehicles will work best. Many bicycle paths or walking paths along lakes may not have adequate room for a bus to get in and out safely (and quickly). The way to move the most people from rest stops to the start/finish is to assign a certain number of SAG(s) to drive exclusively between point A and B and then to "home base" (the start/finish). Others should be assigned to drive exclusively between C and D and "home base," and so on. This way, a vehicle is always within two or three miles from any stop. Once a rest stop has been closed (after the last participant has gone through), the SAGS designated from point A to B can then move on to "sweeping" the route (from A to Z and then back to "home base").

Communications Teams

- Two-way radio communications
- Ham radio communications
- CB radios
- Pay phones/cell phones
- Bull horns

As I've mentioned above, your event will, most likely, be the first time many people will be working together, regardless of pre-event training sessions. Nothing is ever the same as it is on event day. Good communication (equipment and training) is critical to the success of your event. Always expect the unexpected. Once, while managing a walking event in "The Windy City" in early April the temperature reached 87° (about 40° *warmer* than the normal high). At any rate, a young mother was carrying a newborn on her back. The infant became ill and an ambulance had to be called to rush the baby to a nearby hospital. (Everything turned out fine, but if solid communications had not been in place, we could have run into serious problems.)

Two-way radio communications are the best for events with any distance as there is rarely any interruption of service. Daniel J. Lewis, lead engineer for Motorola, the leading manufacturer of two-way radios, states:

> The greatest benefit of two-way radios is that groups of people can talk and listen on the same channel at the same time. With cell phones, however, only two people can talk at the same time. And, as long as radios are kept on, all people with a two-way radio (and people around them) can listen to everything that is happening along a route. Obviously, a cell phone must ring first to communicate.

CBs are adequate for very short distances. They can be very frustrating means of communicating, especially with inexperienced volunteers or staff.

Call your local police department and you're likely to find volunteers with extensive two-way radio experience. It is possible, however, to train your staff to use these. But usually the training is left until the last minute . . . people do not charge the batteries properly, and often misuse is more chaotic than if you had no communications to begin with.

Cell phones are essential for effective communications. It is imperative to have cell phones (or access to pay phones) *at all times* at all key points on the route. In addition, all key staff and medical personnel must be assigned a cell phone. *Be sure to request the cell phone numbers in advance* so you can distribute the night before or day-of with names, titles and locations so that there is no confusion on event day. *Critical note: all vehicles, key staff and volunteers, rest stop volunteers and medical teams must have the same type of communication devices!*

You'll want to place one radio communications person at every rest stop. Then you'll want another person (the one with the most experience) at the start/finish location. Place the communications people near the medical people at all times as they will work as a team. And, most importantly, the event manager *must have a communications tag at all times!* The communications tag person literally follows the event manager around all day long. This is critical to communications effectiveness. Furthermore, it must be clear to all communications people that the event manager is the only one who gives "orders," except in the case of medical emergencies, which must be taken care of immediately.

Bull horns are not replacements for the above, but a welcome addition. They're truly a great "bang for your buck" (they usually run about $11 each). They are helpful in many ways, including crowd control, parking, start/finish ceremonies and in any case of needing to get information to your group.

Hazard Support

Place police or trusted volunteers at all dangerous crossings and streets, especially ones with no traffic lights or intersections known to have a lot of traffic accidents. Police cars are great at hazardous farm roads with no lights because they can turn on their lights. But beware: the first sign of a crisis in a city and they're off like lightning. Your event becomes *low priority!*

Emergency Team

An emergency team is necessary for coordination of any situation which may occur. The team must be composed of top-level staff (especially the PR director or spokesperson), board members or committee volunteers. All contact with the family, media, and hospital should only be handled by this group.

Safety Manual

A safety manual should be prepared for all volunteers. This manual must have tabs for quick retrieval of information (especially in the case of high-risk situations like a heart attack). This booklet should contain the following information:

- Location *and directions* to nearest hospital FROM EACH REST STOP

- Telephone numbers of nearest hospitals
- Detailed maps to nearest hospitals from all points along route
- What to do if . . . (local hospital will provide information on what to do in the case of broken bones, heart attacks, falls, cuts, etc.)
- Telephone numbers of all safety teams
- Telephone numbers to local stores that carry water (in case of shortage)

Supplies Checklist and Banners Distribution

I've run events by the seat of my pants and I've run them prepared. As we all know, prepared is better. Supplies and their distribution is one area where planning is *essential*. I consider supplies to be any non-food item needed for the event. For this list, you'll need a quiet morning away from the office with two other people who know your event as intimately as you do. Look at the sample supplies checklist and banners distribution list in Exhibit 8.3. Naturally, this is only a sample and you'll have to create your own based on your market needs and numbers. Don't let the large numbers scare you . . . it was originally done for a 9,000-person walk! Regardless, it shows you the type of schedule and items you may need.

As far as distribution goes, be very careful how you load your trucks for event day. I'll get into the loading of trucks shortly.

This form can be very helpful in preparing your budget, too. It will give you a good idea of the types of items needed so you can work on their cost and/or get them donated. Many supplies will be donated from a local hospital. But many, unfortunately, will be line items in your budget.

- **Order and pack supplies early.** You don't want to be dividing up supplies the last minute as you load the trucks and/or vans! (Which I've done. Don't do it!) Packing three

SUPPLIES CHECKLIST

	A	B	C	D
REGISTRATION	% of Participants	% of Participants	% of Participants	% of Participants
Pens	400	120	120	120
"I'm Walking For" signs	4000	1100	1100	800
Safety pins	8000	2200	2200	1600
Large black markers	100	35	50	35
Maps	4000	1100	1100	800
$ Envelopes & $ Collection boxes	see accounting	see accounting	see accounting	see accounting
Walker IDs (blank ones for walk-ons)	1000	200	200	200
Garbage boxes	75	25	25	25
T-shirts:				
Regular				
Past Participant				
Team				
Team Past Participant				
Lunch tickets (optional)	4000	1100	1100	800
Heavy tape	10	7	7	7
Finish kits & "goody" bags	4000	1100	1100	800

(Exhibit 8.3) The supplies checklist and banners distribution list will help you think about all the things you'll need for your event — and you won't be caught empty-handed when you need them. The letters A, B, C, and D refer to the different routes of the event.

days in advance is best; you'll have a pretty solid idea of how many participants you'll have and you won't be too harried.

- **Follow your plan for distribution.**
- **Don't forget about the small stuff** . . . like toilet paper and paper towels.

SUPPLIES CHECKLIST

	A	B	C	D
Start-Up & Start Food				
Start/Finish banners	see banner list	see banner list	see banner list	see banner list
Heavy tape	1	1	1	1
Rope	8 large	3 large	8 large	2 large
Route markers & stakes	25	50	20	50
Garbage bags	25	15	15	15
Paper towels	5	2	2	2
Scissors	3	2	2	2
Toilet paper	50	30	30	30
Poster board	4	4	4	4
Large markers	2	2	2	2
Balloons / Arches	arches & balloons	arches only	arches only	balloons only
Extension cord	1		1 -for boombox	
Kleenex	2	1	1	1
Start Food Tables				
Plastic tablecloths	5	2	2	1
Napkins	3 cases	1 case	1 case	3/4 case
Cups for H$_2$O	4,000	1,100	1,100	800
Food gloves	8 pairs	4 pairs	4 pairs	4 pairs
Knives (large)	2	2	2	2
Plastic serving trays	1 sponsor tent	—	—	—
Styrofoam cups (for coffee)	3,000	800	800	600

Pick Up and Delivery of Supplies and Food Schedule

Picking up and delivering your walk supplies and food must be organized beforehand. It sounds simple enough, but I can tell you that not being prepared has thrown everything off. Ideally, you'll want to pick up everything no later than the afternoon before the day of your event. This ensures that everyone gets to

SUPPLIES CHECKLIST

	A	B	C	D
ACCOUNTING				
Pens (ballpoint)	* see registration	* see registration	* see registration	* see registration
6" x 9" envelopes (3 turned in)	2,000	550	550	400
Stapler w/staples	4 (boxes w/ staples)	2 (1 box w/ staples)	2 (1 box w/ staples)	1 (1 box of staples)
Calculator (w/ tape & batteries)	4	2	2	2
Batteries	6 pkgs.	2 pkgs.	2 pkgs.	2 pkgs.
Thank You receipts	15 books	10 books	10 books	10 books
Rubberbands	60	30	30	30
Paper clips	4 boxes	2 boxes	2 boxes	2 books
Legal pads	1	1	1	1
Money collection boxes	35	15	15	15
Scotch tape	5	3	1,100	800
Pre-addressed pledge payment envelopes	4,000	1,100	1,100	800
Return $ envelopes	2,000	550	550	400

their route(s) while there is still daylight to mark the route (in the case of multi-site routes where you may have routes 50 miles away), and staff and volunteers can still get lots of sleep before the BIG DAY.

Be sure to write a delivery/pick-up schedule. Notice the schedule has all the important elements: who, what, where and when. The temptation to wing it is strong, but don't do it!

As you've probably already guessed, you'll need a warehouse facility. As I've mentioned before, a trucking warehouse makes the most sense for storage and ease of loading your truck and/or vans. But if you don't have access, any business that has a **loading dock** will do, depending, of course, on how many routes you have, and how many trucks/vans you have to load and how many supplies need to be loaded. Don't underestimate the space you will need for storage.

SUPPLIES CHECKLIST

	A	B	C	D
VOLUNTEER CHECK-IN				
Volunteer incentive	400	150	125	75
Volunteer lists	•	•	•	•
Job descriptions	•	•	•	•
Lunch tickets	400 +	150 +	125 +	75 +
Maps	425	175	150	100
Pens	5	5	5	5
Legal pad	1	1	1	1
* To be packed by manager of volunteers				
LUNCH				
Garbage bags	40	30	30	40
Paper towels	5	2	5	5
Toilet paper	see start-up list	see start-up list	see start-up list	see start-up list
Plastic tablecloths	20?	—	20?	20?
Plastic gloves	8 pr.	4 pr.	4 pr.	4 pr.
Styrofoam cups (soup)	4000	1,100	1,100	800
Soup spoons	4000	1,100	1,100	800
Knives (LG) & plastic	4000	1,100	1,100	800
Cups	4000	1,100	1,100	800
Napkins	4000	1,100	1,100	800
Signs	4000	1,100	1,100	800
Plates	7	4	4	3
Beverage jugs	4,000	1,100	1,100	1,100

Five Tips for Loading Trucks

I'm no prima donna, but I never thought I'd be driving and loading 36-foot trucks! I've learned a lot over the years. Here are a few tips.

1. **Load farthest routes first** so they can get on the road and have time to mark their routes during daylight.

SUPPLIES CHECKLIST

FIRST AID KITS (If not donated by hospital)	A	B	C	D
ICE PACkS	REST STOP 1=2 2=2 3=2 4=2	S/F 2 BENNET 2 PIANO 2 CLARK 2	S/F 2 GROVE 31 2 ELK PASTURE 2	S/F 2 FOSTER 2
SANITARY NAPKINS	2 2 2 2	S/F 2 BENNET 2 PIANO 2 CLARK 2	S/F 2 GROVE 31 2 ELK PASTURE 2	S/F 2 FOSTER 2
BANDAIDS	4 4 4 4	S/F 2 BENNET 2 PIANO 2 CLARK 2	S/F 2 GROVE 31 2 ELK PASTURE 2	S/F 2 FOSTER 2
HYDROGEN PEROXIDE	2 2 2 2	S/F 2 BENNET 2 PIANO 2 CLARK 2	S/F 2 GROVE 31 2 ELK PASTURE 2	S/F 2 FOSTER 2
ACE BANDAGES	S/F 2 LAKE PT. 2 FULLERTON 2 IRVING 2	S/F 1 BENNET 1 PIANO 1 CLARK 1	S/F 1 GROVE 31 1 ELK PASTURE 1	S/F 1 FOSTER 1

REST STOPS	A	B	C	D
WOODEN/METAL SPOONS	LAKE PT. 1 FULLERTON 1 IRVING 1	FABYAN 1 BENNET 1 PIANO 1 CLARK 1	GROVE 31 1 ELK PASTURE 1	L. FOSTER
TOILET PAPER	LAKE PT. 8 FULLERTON 8 IRVING 8	FABYAN 4 BENNET 4 PIANO 4 CLARK 4	GROVE 31 4 ELK PASTURE 4	L. FOSTER 5
PAPER TOWELS	LAKE PT. 5 FULLERTON 5 IRVING 5	FABYAN 2 BENNET 2 PIANO 2 CLARK 2	GROVE 31 2 ELK PASTURE 2	L. FOSTER 2
PLASTIC TABLECLOTHS	LAKE PT. FULLERTON IRVING	FABYAN BENNET PIANO CLARK	GROVE 31 ELK PASTURE	L. FOSTER
ROPE (for banners)	LAKE PT. 1 FULLERTON 1 IRVING 1			
SCISSORS	LAKE PT. 1 FULLERTON 1 IRVING 1			
CUPS	LAKE PT. 2 FULLERTON 2 IRVING 2	FABYAN BENNET PIANO CLARK	GROVE 31 ELK PASTURE	L. FOSTER
KNIVES	LAKE PT. 4 FULLERTON 4 IRVING 4	FABYAN 4 BENNET 4 PIANO 4 CLARK 4	GROVE 31 4 ELK PASTURE 4	L. FOSTER 4
NAPKINS	LAKE PT. FULLERTON IRVING	FABYAN BENNET PIANO CLARK	GROVE 31 ELK PASTURE	L. FOSTER
CUTTING TRAYS	LAKE PT. 6 FULLERTON 6 IRVING 6	FABYAN 3 BENNET 3 PIANO 3 CLARK 3	GROVE 31 3 ELK PASTURE 3	L. FOSTER 3
GARBAGE BAGS	LAKE PT. 20 FULLERTON 20 IRVING 20	FABYAN 10 BENNET 10 PIANO 10 CLARK 10	GROVE 31 15 ELK PASTURE 15	L. FOSTER 20
PLASTIC GLOVES	LAKE PT. FULLERTON IRVING	FABYAN 4 PR BENNET 4 PR PIANO 4 PR CLARK 4 PR	GROVE 31 4 PR ELK PASTURE 4 PR	L. FOSTER 4 PR
KLEENEX	LAKE PT. 2 FULLERTON 2 IRVING 2	FABYAN 1 BENNET 1 PIANO 1 CLARK 1	GROVE 31 1 ELK PASTURE 1	L. . FOSTER 1
HEAVY TAPE	LAKE PT. 1 FULLERTON 1 IRVING 1	FABYAN 1 BENNET 1 PIANO 1 CLARK 1	GROVE 31 1 ELK PASTURE 1	L. FOSTER 1
GATORADE JUGS	LAKE PT. 1 FULLERTON 1 IRVING 1	FABYAN 1 BENNET 1 PIANO 1 CLARK 1	GROVE 31 1 ELK PASTURE 1	L. FOSTER 1

2. **Load LAST STOP FIRST!** (FIRST IN, LAST OUT). My first time loading a truck I loaded my first rest stop in the *back* of the truck and so on and so on . . . well, you know what happened. The morning of the event my route volunteers were dropping off rest stop supplies and food which had been carefully marked and color-coded by stop. Only one thing wrong. They had to unload the truck at the first stop to get to the back of the truck to unload the right supplies!

	A	B	C	D
BANNERS DISTRIBUTION LIST				
START/FINISH	·	·	·	·
Pledge payment registration	✓	✓	✓	✓
Non-payment registration	✓	✓	✓	✓
Team registration	✓	✓	✓	✓
Medical	✓	✓	✓	✓
Finish line check-in	✓	✓	✓	✓
Sponsor tent	✓	✓	✓	✓
Volunteer check-in	✓	✓	✓	✓
Cause/mission banner	✓	✓	✓	✓
Information signs	✓	✓	✓	✓
Team meeting area	✓	✓	✓	✓
Sponsor banner	2	1	1	1
START/FINISH banner	✓	✓	✓	✓

3. **Recruit strong volunteers.** Sorry, but this is one job most women can't do. If you know women who bodybuild, great. But if not, get some young, strong and responsible male volunteers. Male staff work best if you can spare them. The worst feeling in the morning is having a supply truck, but no one to drive and/or unload. And always have a car available to follow the truck around with manpower. This is hard work at five or six a.m.!

4. **Hire loading help.** This is one place you can't scrimp and save. Don't wear out your day-of-event volunteers and staff by over-taxing them. Sure they need to be there. Their role on loading day is to direct supplies and food into the truck in the proper order and amount.

5. **Color-code all boxes and all routes before you get to the loading facility.** If you have two walk routes, pick two different colors. Assign one color per route. Place a colored square on both sides of your route's truck. Then, assign different colors for each of your rest stops (red = rest stop 1; blue = rest stop 2, etc.). Tape a piece of the assigned colored paper to each and every box for each rest stop. This way, it will be easier to load — and,

more importantly, to unload the right supplies and amounts of food at the rest stops at five or six a.m.

Bells and Whistles

Bells and whistles are all the frills of your event — they can set you apart from your competition. Bells and whistles are balloons and balloon arches, entertainment, pre-walk warm-ups, celebrities, music and, of course, finish-line cheerers. But, most of all, bells and whistles can help tie your cause to your event! Incorporate education in start speeches by clients or patients or important community leaders. If you have a health-related cause, ask a client to speak about his/her disease in a positive way, helping personalize the disease.

Bells and whistles are not limited by your budget. There are many local theater groups and health clubs that are more than happy to come out and help "get things going." Get your sponsors involved, too. Perhaps they have a mascot? Keebler Cookies has a huge blow-up Ernie the Elf that helps make an event festive; White Castle hamburgers has a larger-than-life hamburger; Subway subs has a human sub-sandwich! Nestea Iced tea has an enormous traveling ad with a roving beverage cart.

Frills are important. They make the event a happening, tie the event to your cause and thank the participants by giving something back for their efforts.

Pre-, Day-of, and Post-Event Timeline

Two Days Before Event

- Call park districts reminding them of the walk. Make sure they have all gates open early for truck deliveries to rest stops.
- Contact city, village or town police, Streets and Sanitation, etc.

- Food pick-up/delivery coordinator to orchestrate last minute pick-up of all items, if needed.
- Meet at office to have one last briefing session on last minute changes and to distribute communications (hold training session on usage).
- Go home early.
- Relax!

Day Before Event

- Confirm with ALL vendors, especially tents, port-a-potties, etc.
- Drive to trucking/van rental facility (if renting trucks) at nine a.m.
- Meet at loading dock of warehousing facility.
- Load trucks farthest route out first.
- Check out route and mark it late in day (or assign to volunteers).
- Relax. Have a beer. Have only one beer!

Event Day

Note: As the route manager, you should never touch a box. You are the manager and must remain focused on the big picture.

- Arrive at site no later than one and a half hours before event start time. (I recommend starting registration at 7:30 with a 9:00 a.m. start).
- Set up "volunteer day-of check-in" *first* so your early morning volunteers can be assigned!
- Rental items, such as tables and chairs are often dropped at the start/finish site and transferred by a "rover" van to stops.
- Send a "rover" van to all rest stops with a pre-assigned number of tables and chairs. It *must* get there before the rest stop supply truck gets there. A rover van is a van filled with extra supplies of everything. It is usually a cargo van (a van that has no rear seats) which can easily maneuver

into and out of rest stop areas. When a rest stop is running out of water, for example, a rest stop captain can radio for more water. It is imperative that the rover van driver be in communication with rest stops at all times.

- Send out supplies/food rest stop delivery truck with strong unloaders.
- Pre-assigned volunteer to bring coffee, juice and muffins for all volunteers. For large sites where you may have hundreds of volunteers, you'll need to have this catered.
- Unload all registration materials and banners *first* (I usually keep them in the cab of the truck with me if there is room).
- Give banners to banner team to hang immediately.
- Set up registration tables (again, delegate — a pre-assigned, pre-trained registration captain should handle everything!).
- Take a deep breath and enjoy the day!

Post-Event

Monday After

- Send all pledge "invoices."
- Return all vehicles, tables, chairs, etc.
- Input pledge totals into your computer system.
- Mail "we missed you" letters to no-shows (see Exhibit 8.4).

Wednesday After

Compile the following statistics:

- Number of pre-registrants
- Number of walk-ons
- Number of no-shows
- Number of walkers
- Total dollars in pledges
- Total paid to date
- Total sponsorship dollars

PLEDGE PLEA TO "NO-SHOWS"

EVENT LETTERHEAD OR "TEMPLATE" HERE

DATE AFTER EVENT

Dear Friend

We missed you! We are sorry you couldn't make it on (date of event) for the
(name of event). However, that doesn't mean you can't STILL participate!

You probably worked hard collecting lots of pledges and we're disappointed
that you couldn't make it, but you can still qualify for prizes, just walk in your
neighborhood — along your favorite path. It needn't be as far..

Many critical services for our patients/clients/organization are sustained by
fundraising events such as the (your event name here). Without your energy
and support, many services/people would suffer.

We've enclosed a prize form and a postage-paid envelope for you to return your
pledges.

Sincerely,

Susan Briggs
WLK-TV CBS
Honorary Walk Chairperson

PS. If you did walk, and we sent you this letter in error, please accept our
sincerest apologies — thanks for walking!

(Exhibit 8.4) Send this letter to no-shows — everyone who pre-registered but didn't show up for the event. You might be able to recover some pledges.

Day-of Manual

The day-of manual is an absolute necessity. Here's what it should contain:

- A list of all participants
- Accounting and registration procedures
- Telephone numbers of *all key staff and volunteers*

- Contact names/telephone numbers of all vendors
- Telephone numbers of all other route managers (if you have multiple routes)
- A copy of the safety manual
- Cell phone and radio communications instructions
- Detailed day-of timeline
- Greeting script and PR timeline for morning introductions, thank-yous (to participants and sponsors) and information about the cause
- Many copies of the route map
- Many detailed copies of your site plan (set-up of site, noting location of each and every banner, table, chair, toilet, etc. See Exhibit 8.5.)
- Insurance confirmations and permits

Volunteer Job Descriptions

The following are *samples* of specific job descriptions for a general walk route. *They must be tailored to meet your unique route and volunteers.*

Logistics Set-Up and Rover

NAME _____

JOB LOCATION _____

VOLUNTEER CHECK-IN LOCATION _____

TIME _____

1. Supervise tent, table and chair set-up.
2. Supervise hanging banners and signs.
3. Supervise placement of route markers up to one mile along path from start/finish banner.
4. Ensure that toilet paper is in all port-a-potties.
5. After complete set-up, go to rest stops, using a cargo van, to drop off initial supplies and greet volunteers. After the event begins, continue monitoring rest stops for supply deficiencies and respond to requests for additional supplies.

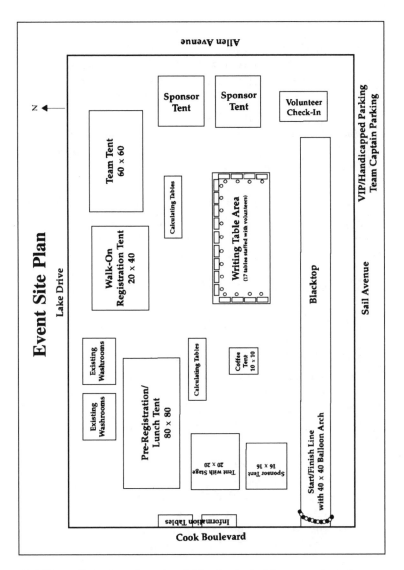

(Exhibit 8.5) A site plan should be included in your day-of-event manual. Note the location of every element in your event, no matter how trivial, down to the last chair.

6. Stay in contact with the rest stops through the communications person (person with radio or phone) to replenish supplies as needed (pick up additional supplies for lunch if needed), comfort and thank volunteers and communicate transportation

needs to buses (tell the communications person to radio for bus if you have participants that need to be picked up).

7. As the event comes to an end, communicate traffic flow to registration managers and site manager. Monitor route to make sure you don't leave participants without transportation and support.

8. Let rest stop volunteers know when to close down rest stops and assist them as needed. Make sure that locations are left as clean as possible and that all supplies are loaded on your van. Leave the tables and chairs and the tents. The rental company will pick them up.

The trash should be bagged by the volunteers as the day goes by and stacked neatly for the Parks Department to pick up. If possible, have the volunteers keep the cans separate.

Parking Attendant

NAME _____

JOB LOCATION _____

VOLUNTEER CHECK-IN LOCATION _____

TIME _____

1. Smile!

2. Direct cars into spaces — we do not want to block in anyone!

3. Save spaces closest to registration as handicapped spaces and for VIPs and top fund raisers.

4. If people have questions about where they should go, send them to a **greeter.** (Greeters should be placed just after people leave their cars and are walking into the walk start area.)

5. THANK YOU for your fight against (name of cause here).

Breakfast Server

NAME _____

JOB LOCATION _____

VOLUNTEER CHECK-IN LOCATION _____

TIME _____

1. SMILE !

2. Slice up any cake or muffins in pieces. Please do not open boxes before you need them — we must ensure the quality of the cakes for our sponsor(s).

3. Place on napkin — serve.

4. Please keep area clean of paper trash.

5. THANK YOU for your fight against (name of cause here).

Check-in Table Volunteer

NAME _____
JOB LOCATION _____
VOLUNTEER CHECK-IN LOCATION _____
TIME _____

1. SMILE! Thank them for coming.

2. Ask for each volunteers name and cross/check it off the list.

3. Ask volunteers to complete their emergency ID form.

4. Give volunteers their lunch tickets and route maps.

5. Direct volunteers to their volunteer location.

Thank you for volunteering!

Greeter

NAME _____
JOB LOCATION _____
VOLUNTEER CHECK-IN LOCATION _____
TIME _____

1. SMILE!

2. Welcome participants. Use phrases like: "Good morning," "thank you for coming," and, "have a good time."

3. Very important: Please direct *all* walkers (or cyclists) to the writing tables before they go to any registration area! It is very important to direct *all* walkers to the writing tables to prevent

chaos at registration. The walkers will be given all the necessary registration information at the writing tables.

4. Participants will then proceed to their proper check-in area. Tents will be marked "Non-Payment Registration," "Pledge Payment Registration" or "Team Registration."

Thank you for volunteering!

Writing Table Volunteer

NAME _____

JOB LOCATION _____

VOLUNTEER CHECK-IN LOCATION _____

TIME _____

The purpose of the writing table volunteer is to serve as a trouble shooter by answering walkers' questions and to make sure *all* walkers have their registration materials prepared before approaching any registration area. This will ensure a smooth registration process.

1. Welcome walkers.

2. Give walker a walker "bib number" and have them complete their emergency information on the back. A "bib number," a.k.a. a "race number," is a number which corresponds to each participant. Walkers wear "bib numbers" on their front, while cyclists wear their numbers on their backs (due to wind). Emergency information (name of doctor, who to call in the case of an emergency, etc., is always on the back of the "bib").

3. Make sure walkers complete emergency information!

4. Ask walkers if they have their walker ID cards.

If yes, direct walkers to appropriate registration areas: team registration, pledge payment registration, non-payment registration.

If no, give walker a walker ID form and check the walk-on box.

5. Direct walker to correct registration area: team registration, pledge payment registration, non-payment registration.

6. Give all walk-ons a walker ID card to fill out.

7. Serve as a troubleshooter — answer any questions walkers may have.

Thank you for volunteering!

Pledge Payment Registration Volunteer

NAME _____

JOB LOCATION _____

VOLUNTEER CHECK-IN LOCATION _____

TIME _____

1. Welcome walkers with a smile!

2. Make sure walkers have already been to the writing table.

3. Ask walkers if they are part of a walk team. If yes, direct them to the team registration area.

4. Ask walkers for their walker IDs.

5. Make sure walker IDs are completed and legible: name, address, phone number. (Make sure waivers are signed.)

6. Ask walkers to fill in the three boxes on the top left corner of the walker ID (pledged amount, pledges turned in the day of event and any balance due).

7. Have walkers initial the amount of pledge money turned in.

8. Collect money from walkers and initial the amount of pledge money turned in on the walker IDs.

9. Ask walkers if they are club members, e.g., walk veterans or top fund raisers. (Anyone who has participated in the walk before.)

10. If walkers turn in $X amount or more, they receive a t-shirt. Circle t-shirt size on walker ID card (if prize form is combined with walker ID) and tell t-shirt runner what size and type of t-shirt you need.

11. Give receipt to walkers.

12. Seal envelope containing the money and place in box at your station.

13. Ensure that emergency information is completed and hand walkers two safety pins to secure their "bib numbers."

14. Hand walkers their lunch tickets.

15. Wish walkers *good luck!*

Thank you for volunteering!

Non-Payment Registration Volunteer

NAME _____

JOB LOCATION _____

VOLUNTEER CHECK-IN LOCATION _____

TIME _____

    1. Make sure walker ID is completed and legible: name, address, phone number should be clear. (Make sure waiver is signed.) See Exhibit 8.6 for a sample of a walker ID.

    2. Suggest to walkers in a *friendly tone* a minimum pledge of $25.00. Write initial amount of pledge money turned in on walker ID.

SAMPLE WALKER IDENTIFICATION (I.D.) CARD

Walker Identification Card

name_____

address_____

city_____

state_____ zip_____

home phone (   )_____

work phone (   )_____

TOTAL PLEDGE	$
Amount Turned In	$
Balance Due	$
Verified by	*(volunteer signature here)*

YOU MUST TURN
THIS CARD IN ON _____ *(event date here)*

WAIVER

I hereby waive all claims against the (your charity event name here), its sponsors or any personnel for any injury I might suffer in this event. I attest that I am physically fit and prepared for this event. I grant full permission for organizers to use photographs of me and quotations from me in legitimate accounts and promotions of this event.

_____
signature

_____
parent or guardian's signature if less than 18 years of age.

Include this card in second participant mailing

(Exhibit 8.6) The walker identification card should address the basics (name, address, phone, etc.), but you can also put the prize selection form on the back. It all depends on your system. Don't forget the hold-harmless waiver.

3. Ask walkers to fill in top three boxes on top left corner of walker ID.

4. Also remind walkers they have one month, until X date, to turn in their pledges. If a walker turns in $X amount, he or she will receive a *great* walk t-shirt!

5. Ensure that emergency information is complete and hand walker two safety pins.

6. Hand each walker his or her lunch ticket.

7. Wish walkers *good luck!*

Thank you for volunteering!

T-Shirt Table Volunteer

NAME _____

JOB LOCATION _____

VOLUNTEER CHECK-IN LOCATION _____

TIME _____

Each walker is given a t-shirt if he or she turns in a minimum of $X in pledges the day of the walk. Walkers who do not turn in a minimum of $X in pledges will receive a t-shirt through the mail if they send in a minimum of $X in pledges before the payment deadline of (insert date here).

1. You will be working as a team with the registrar to retrieve t-shirts in the registration area.

Please note: Walker must receive the t-shirt size he or she pre-ordered so we have enough for everyone!

2. Hand walker his or her t-shirt.

3. Wish walker *good luck*!

Thank you for volunteering!

Rest Stop Volunteer

NAME _____

JOB LOCATION _____

VOLUNTEER CHECK-IN LOCATION _____

TIME _____

The rest stops are the communications, safety and support headquarters of the walk. Express support for the walkers as they approach your stop. A smile goes a long way!

Please be sure to report to volunteer check-in before arriving at your assigned rest stop.

1. Assist in setting up tables, signs, banners, food, drinks and trash bags.

2. Cut fruit up into quarters. Put water in cups and line up on the tables before walkers arrive.

3. Keep refreshments replenished throughout the walk. Have water poured into cups and ready when walkers arrive.

4. Cheer walkers on as they resume walking. Do not allow walkers to congregate for too long. We want them to keep moving so that their muscles don't cramp!

5. Assist with taking down and cleaning up the rest stop area.

Notes:

- There will be a first aid person and a communications member assigned to every rest stop. Direct any injuries to the first aid person and radio for assistance if needed.
- Things sometimes get slow. Bring a radio along to keep you company (it also helps keep the walkers' feet moving!).
- Bring rain gear in case of bad weather. The walk will take place come rain or shine!
- Send a runner to the lunch stop to pick up sandwiches for your rest stop volunteers.

Thank you for volunteering!

Rest Stop Captain

NAME _____

JOB LOCATION _____

VOLUNTEER CHECK-IN LOCATION _____

TIME _____

It is extremely important that you are friendly, helpful and enthusiastic. Express support for the walkers. A smile goes a long way! The walkers are "customers" for the day and we want them to enjoy the experience and tell their friends about it so that they will walk next year.

Please be sure to report to volunteer check-in before you arrive at your assigned rest stop location.

The rest stops are the communications, safety and support headquarters of the walk. In case of an emergency, you will be in charge of coordinating the medical team and radio communications people.

1. After reporting to volunteer check-in, go directly to your assigned rest stop. Do not stay at volunteer check-in for the start of the walk.

2. Set up the rest stop. Use your imagination and creativity to make it interesting!

3. Cut all fruit into quarters.

4. Keep refreshments replenished throughout the walk; have water poured into cups and ready when walkers arrive.

5. Make sure port-a-potties have toilet paper.

6. Keep area clean and free of loose paper.

7. You should have four to five volunteers to assist you.

8. After all walkers have passed and the area is clean, radio for equipment pick-up. A van will come by to load any leftover food and supplies.

9. Report to finish and welcome the remaining walkers!

Note: In case of an emergency, notify your communications person to radio for help.

Thank you for volunteering!

Lunch Service Volunteer

NAME _____

JOB LOCATION _____

VOLUNTEER CHECK-IN LOCATION _____

TIME _____

1. Set up tables, chairs and food service under direction of lunch captain.

2. Welcome weary walkers with a smile!

3. Ask walkers for their lunch tickets. Note: In the case of cycling events, the lunch ticket is often a special order tear-off coupon located on their "bib numbers."

4. Serve only one serving; we need to have enough food for *all walkers* and volunteers.

5. Please keep area clean of paper trash. Separate cans and juice boxes if possible.

Thank you for volunteering!

Goody Bag Distributor/ Cheering Volunteer

NAME _____

JOB LOCATION _____

VOLUNTEER CHECK-IN LOCATION _____

TIME _____

1. Smile and clap a lot! Say phrases like, "Way to go!" "Great job!" "Thank you!" You will be provided with a horn and streamers!

2. Congratulate walkers.

3. Hand each walker a goody bag which contains his or her completion packet. If you haven't incorporated prize selection in the walker ID, the completion packet should include a prize selection form (see Exhibit 8.7).

4. Hand any required loose ads, coupons, products to walkers.

Thank you for volunteering!

Staff Structure and Management

Every person within an organization should have a role in the walk, regardless of that person's department or knowledge of pledge-based events. Of course, you will want to match up abilities, skills and interests with available walk "positions." Naturally, this decision can only be made from the executive director level or it will create chaos within an organization. Regardless,

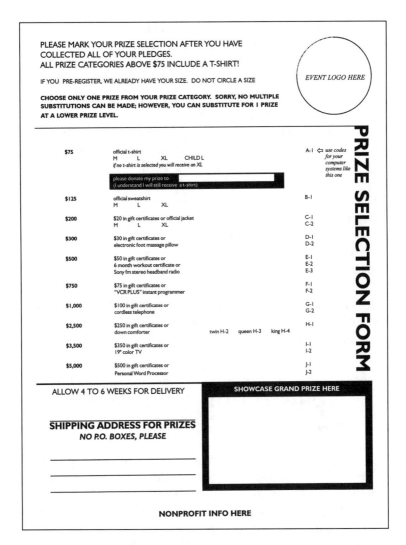

PLEASE MARK YOUR PRIZE SELECTION AFTER YOU HAVE
COLLECTED ALL OF YOUR PLEDGES.
ALL PRIZE CATEGORIES ABOVE $75 INCLUDE A T-SHIRT!

IF YOU PRE-REGISTER, WE ALREADY HAVE YOUR SIZE. DO NOT CIRCLE A SIZE

EVENT LOGO HERE

CHOOSE ONLY ONE PRIZE FROM YOUR PRIZE CATEGORY. SORRY, NO MULTIPLE
SUBSTITUTIONS CAN BE MADE; HOWEVER, YOU CAN SUBSTITUTE FOR 1 PRIZE
AT A LOWER PRIZE LEVEL.

$75	official t-shirt M L XL CHILD L *if no t-shirt is selected you will receive an XL*	A-1 ⇦ *use codes* *for your* *computer* *systems like* *this one*
	please donate my prize to (I understand I will still receive a t-shirt)	
$125	official sweatshirt M L XL	B-1
$200	$20 in gift certificates or official jacket M L XL	C-1 C-2
$300	$30 in gift certificates or electronic foot massage pillow	D-1 D-2
$500	$50 in gift certificates or 6 month workout certificate or Sony fm stereo headband radio	E-1 E-2 E-3
$750	$75 in gift certificates or "VCR PLUS" instant programmer	F-1 F-2
$1,000	$100 in gift certificates or cordless telephone	G-1 G-2
$2,500	$250 in gift certificates or down comforter twin H-2 queen H-3 king H-4	H-1
$3,500	$350 in gift certificates or 19" color TV	I-1 I-2
$5,000	$500 in gift certificates or Personal Word Processor	J-1 J-2

PRIZE SELECTION FORM

ALLOW 4 TO 6 WEEKS FOR DELIVERY

SHOWCASE GRAND PRIZE HERE

SHIPPING ADDRESS FOR PRIZES
NO P.O. BOXES, PLEASE

NONPROFIT INFO HERE

(Exhibit 8.7) Include the prize selection form in the completion packet. Use computer codes to make your prize fulfillment easier. Specify street addresses only because you'll probably be sending your prizes via UPS — and they don't deliver to post office boxes.

some employees will feel they are being forced into doing something they may not want to do, and some will feel it is a privilege to be asked. One of the trickiest things to do is to get ongoing support from internal staff, specifically employees who already have a "full plate" as they say. But, be forewarned: let your staff know early about this commitment and keep them informed through walk updates (an internal newsletter if you will), monthly memorandums and updates at all staff meetings.

Next, list all employees on the vertical side of a spreadsheet and all available positions horizontally. Highlight the most important positions first, such as route manager, registration manager, etc. You'll naturally want to put any available development people in these positions. Next, place management in the next most important positions, and so on. Place employees who are not as responsible (ones who are habitually late) in less critical roles (e.g., clean-up). However, it is always a good idea to request that *all* staff arrive at six a.m. to help set up, regardless of their role. For most employees, this will be a once-a-year deal — it's not too much to ask.

As I mentioned above, it is critical that you keep *all* your staff informed at all junctures. Have regular walk staff meetings, monthly at first, more often as you get closer to event day. This seems elementary, but communication within your organization will be the first to fall apart. This creates dissension and frustration at the time you'll need it least.

Registration Procedures and Training

Below is a sample registration process for the day of your event. Please note, this is for example only and your registration process must be carefully tailored to your event and systems capabilities. Registration processes for walks and for other kinds of events vary greatly. There are forms with several copies of the pledge sheet, and there are forms which have only one copy and the walker must copy his or her forms for his or her records and to collect pledges. The latter is preferred because it saves a considerable amount of money for the nonprofit.

I recommend that the following stations be set up to accommodate your participants (some of these stations can be combined depending on how many walkers each site is expecting):

Station 1: Writing Table. Have separate tables for participants who need to complete paperwork. Day-of registrants will need this area to complete registration forms and pledge sheets. Be sure to have volunteers stationed to answer questions and to direct walkers to appropriate stations.

Station 2: Pre-Registered Walkers. Participants who have registered prior to the day of the event should be directed to this area. You should separate this station by the alphabet: A-M, N-Z, etc. (depending on the number of walkers, you may need to separate further). At this station, pre-registered participants will check in and submit their pledge sheets.

Station 3: Day-of Registration. Walkers who are registering on the day of the event should be directed to this station upon completing paperwork at station 1. Collect a *copy* of the pledge sheet and attach it to the completed registration form.

Station 4: Team Registration. This station is much the same as station 2. Pre-registered teams will check in and submit a copy of their pledge sheet. A designated check-in area for teams can be promoted as an incentive for forming a team.

Recommended Registration Process for Stations 2 to 4: *Each station should be provided with a list of pre-registered walkers/teams.

1. If the participants are pre-registered, check their names off the list.

2. Each walker must present a pledge sheet (the walker can sign a new one if he or she forgets it). Make sure the walker indicates a prize category (if applicable to your form — some walker IDs can be combined with prize forms. It's all up to your system).

3. It is helpful if the pledge sheets provided to participants are in duplicate. But, as stated above, it is a lot more expensive to do it this way. If that is the case, make sure you stress to the walkers in all pre-event newsletters to *copy their pledge forms.* If walkers do not copy their forms and they turn them in, they will not have records of who sponsored them and for how much!

4. If a walker is turning in money, please insert the money and a copy of the pledge sheet(s) into a #10 envelope.

5. If your walkers are eligible for a t-shirt, each station should have stock or, after being checked in, walkers should be directed to a separate t-shirt table.

Suggestions:

- Each station should have a box or container to hold paperwork. The volunteers can insert each participant's paperwork/money into the box and this should reduce the chance of lost paperwork and/or money.
- To encourage participants to turn in pledges on the day of the event, issue t-shirts only to those walkers turning in pledges of X amount (and, again, this must be advertised in pre-event communication pieces, especially the newsletter).
- Assign a volunteer to act as the registration "captain." This person will monitor the stations, act as the trouble-shooter, and add volunteers as needed.

What If . . . ? A Guide to Plan B

Most insurance underwriters will request a safety plan containing your detailed plan for potential crisis. Regardless, a Plan B is just plain smart. First, you'll want to ensure a safe walk. Second, you'll want to collect pledges, regardless of whether or not the walk takes place. So on a number of fronts, pre-planning is important or you're setting up your organization for possible disaster.

Should your event go on rain or shine? I say yes. Rain, shine — even snow. I've done walks in the rain, snow and even bitter cold. Most often, people know the weather situation before they leave home. However, you must draw the line at safety. If the weather in any way can jeopardize your walkers, you must post-pone a few hours, re-schedule or even cancel.

Consequences of severe weather for a walk are simply not the same as on a long-distance bicycle tour (as a walk route is much shorter and it can be monitored more easily); however, they are nonetheless as important. Here's an abridged version of a real-life two-day bicycle tour that didn't have a Plan B:

Nearly 1,700 cyclists biked nearly 90 miles the first day, up rolling hills under the hot sun (92°). The first day was tough, but they all made it. Overnight, a huge storm rolled in. I monitored the storm through the National Weather Service and it didn't look like the rain was going to stop by the next morning. It didn't. It rained and rained *and rained*. Volunteers did not show up, including radio operators. Therefore, we did not know if we even had a "safe" route, e.g., were bridges out? Streets flooded? When the cyclists finally woke at five a.m., it was still raining. We did not have a Plan B. There were a number of potential problems brewing. Some cyclists began cycling on the slick pavement (although we shouted warnings that the tour was postponed until the rain stopped and the route was secure with volunteers, rest stops, etc.). We had another 1,200 people asking questions and we had no answers. And, worst of all, the gym in which we held breakfast was too small to fit everyone in at the same time so it was hot and way overcrowded. This created a near mutiny situation. In the meantime, we threw together a "crisis team" and determined our options. At the time, we thought it was best to offer people the option to be bused home with their bicycles back to the city, some 90 miles north. But it was Sunday morning in a small town; where would we find enough trucks to hold the bicycles? We called the police, located a rental truck company, woke the owner up and recruited truck drivers from staff. Our luggage truck became our bicycle transport truck and our buses were called in off the route to haul people to the start/finish. By 11 a.m. the sun came out and it was a beautiful day. Eight hundred people had already taken the bus option with another 400 or so setting off to ride (but leaving so late in the day meant some would be riding in the dark on their way home). Luckily, enough volunteers showed up at the rest stops to make it safe and we were able to pick up the riders who weren't finished before dark). It turned out okay (no one was hurt), but it was rough on everyone. Worst of all, we lost future participants, as many would never return to ride with us again, and we created a situation where the participants rode less distance, which could have affected their pledge collection. In addition, some lost faith in us and questioned our ability to direct their hard-earned funds to the right place. **Moral of the story:** A good Plan B not only ensures the physical safety of your participants, but it insures the financial safety of your event as well.

To avoid the above consequences, prepare a detailed plan well before event day. Here are a few tips:

1. Garner media support *before* event day. Ask them to be your partners in an "early warning system," notifying walkers early in the morning about event re-scheduling or cancellation.

Advise walkers through pre-event newsletters on where to tune in for day-of event information.

2. Talk to bus company owners and arrange to call them on an as-needed basis in case the severe weather doesn't start until walkers are already on their way. Usually they can round up drivers even on short notice. Often, your SAG vehicles will be enough to transport people back to the start/finish area, but be prepared.

3. Ask yourself the following questions:

- What is the chain of command? Who cancels an event and when?
- If an event needs to be canceled after participants are out on the route, how many buses or vans will I need?
- How will we stop walkers already on the route? (Believe it or not, many people will refuse to stop.)
- How will we collect pledges if the event is canceled?

Regarding the collection of pledges after an event is canceled: I have found that a well-written pre-planned direct mail piece and personalized calls to all registrants have yielded good results. You won't collect 100% of pledges, but you'll be in the ballgame (about 70% to 85%).

Nine

The Definitive Word on Corporate Sponsorships

As I'm sure you've learned through other areas of development and management in general, we learn from asking the professionals who do it best. As I mentioned in the introduction, we need to take nonprofit events out of the "mom and pop" arena and run our events like businesses. Two of the best sponsorship marketing people I have had the opportunity to work with are Kim Glasman and Glen Ryniewski. Kim is director of marketing for Country Thunder USA, a popular country western venue in Wisconsin, which is host to national concerts. Glen is the sponsorship and media director for the City of Chicago Mayor's Office of Special Events, which puts on the single largest special event in the world, The Taste of Chicago. Kim and Glen have contributed ideas, concepts and strategies to this chapter — all from non-walking events — which can impact your walk as well as other campaigns significantly.

Selling Your Event

In this day of reduced nonprofit budgets, the best way to build your budget for events is to sell sponsorships. Fortunately, sports sponsorship is one of the hottest marketing tools for non-profits. Major companies have large budgets dedicated for sports sponsorships. The hard part is figuring out how to get a share of the pie for your event.

The first step is to identify and understand the companies who will provide sponsorship. It doesn't make sense to attempt to sell a sponsorship to a company that will gain no benefit from exposure to your market.

Before you can do this, you need to identify your participants. Determine the buying characteristics of the people who will attend your event. What products will they buy? What are their likes and dislikes? (For more on this, see the "Demographics" section on page 154.) Is your event being held in a resort town with a highly transient population? Obviously, it would not make sense to sell a sponsorship to a mortgage lender or real estate firm. Is the event a walk in a residential area which is attended by a large number of local residents? Try a grocery store chain or popular retailer (especially since they can get "cooperative money" from the lines they carry). Begin by making a list of companies that match the buying habits of *your* target audience.

The Proposal

The next step is writing a proposal. The proposal should include key points about your event: past attendance, location, dates and times, advertising information. It must include information on how many people will attend, how much exposure the sponsors will receive and how it will increase the traffic and sales for their businesses. If you want to entice national sponsors you must demonstrate to them how they are going to be able to move more products through their local distributor or outlet. Your proposal should be a clear and concise tool to solicit sponsors. It should include quantitative information regarding the benefit to the sponsor. For example, if you are trying to bring on a major soft drink as a sponsor for your walk, some of the benefits to the sponsor would be tagging their logo on all of your advertising and promotional material, providing they are the exclusive beverage served at the event, in cups sporting their logo and including their banners and product displays on the course. Additionally, and here is the key, present a way of cross-promoting with *their* retailers. For example, you could say in your advertising that pledge forms can be picked up at the ABC cola display at all Joe's Supermarkets in town.

Important things to remember:

- Corporations get thousands of sponsorship proposals. Yours must be professionally produced and provide enough value to the sponsor.
- Corporations have their own lists of criteria on which they base decisions. Ask what types of things they like to see in a proposal.
- Do not simply send out proposals randomly. This is a very involved process and must be approached at a personal level. Make sure you speak to the person who will review the proposal to learn if there is a potential "fit." Your objective should be to learn what the sponsor *needs* and *expects* for a successful sponsorship.

A big sponsorship myth is that sponsorships always come out of the marketing department. Not always. Many sponsorships come out of community affairs, public relations, even governmental affairs (depending on your cause). If one area does not have the budget or is not interested, don't give up — ask to speak to another area within the same corporation. Different departments have different needs. The Mercedes Benz PR department sponsored a walking event I managed. Even though I made the ask, I was a bit surprised. Why would a luxury foreign car manufacturer be interested in sponsoring a walking event whose participants have an average family income of $50,000 (far less than their target of $75,000)? Because they were foreign and wanted a good community presence. They wanted to give something back. Incidentally, it worked great: Mercedes provided their luxury cars (driven by employees) to be used as SAG vehicles, actually picking up weary walkers. Additionally, Mercedes promoted the event to their employees and sponsored a team. Even the vice president got into the action. The employees were thrilled to be part of a community event, the top brass were pleased with the internal and external PR and media coverage and we were thrilled with an ongoing partnership that grew over the years.

Demographics

Before you will be able to target potential sponsors, you will need to know who your *own* audience is. What is their median age? What percentage is male and what percentage is female? Are they college graduates? Knowing who your participants are is the most important piece of information you can give to a sponsor. If this is the first time you are doing a walk, you'll want to let your sponsor know who you are targeting to participate. As I spoke of earlier in Chapter 4, once you have completed the first year and have captured the demographic data (from registration forms, surveys, etc.), you will have the important information your sponsors will want to know.

Participant Demographic Information

- Median age
- Median income
- Gender
- Education
- Children
- Household income
- Household composition (single mom, single dad, etc.)
- Home ownership and value

You can get very specific. In fact, the more specific you get, the easier it is to find sponsors. For example, your data shows that 63% of all participants bought a foreign new car in the last two years. This is a strong signal to target *foreign* new car dealers as a **title** or **presenting sponsor.**

To get the specific data you must request as much information as you can on your registration form. However, there is a limit to how much people will fill out (as well as space constraints). Therefore, the best way to capture this data is through a walker survey *on event day.* (Naturally, this only works for future years' proposals. If this is a first-year event, look to similar, perhaps competitive, events to get a general idea of who your participants will be.) The best time to "get" the walkers is just after registration and before the start of the walk (give out a survey at registration and have big boxes at the start line to turn in) or shortly after they have crossed the finish line. Here are some specific questions you'll want to ask (I recommend consulting with a marketing research firm to actually write the questions, tabulate and report back):

> What types of activities do you regularly participate in?
> How many times a week do you walk?
> Do you walk for exercise?
> Why are you participating in the XYZ Walk?
> How did you hear about the XYZ Walk?
> What types of clothing do you purchase in stores?
> What types by mail?
> Would you like catalogs from our sponsors?
> What credit cards have you used in the past two months?
> Have you been to Europe?
> What is your favorite vacation destination?
> Do you rent cars?
> Who do you most often travel with?
> How likely would you be to purchase a product by (name of sponsor(s)) simply because they sponsored the event?
> Other comments:

In addition to walker surveys and information on registration forms, depending on the sophistication of your computer system, you may want to consider contacting an information provider such as R.R. Donnelley. R.R. Donnelley and many other providers have specific programs which can match the data on your participants (based on the zip code in which they live) and then group them into "clusters" or groups. It is the only way to get precise demographic and lifestyle data on your participants *and people who are similar to your participants.* For example, let's say that the single largest number of your participants comes from zip code 60611 (downtown Chicago). The information provider will categorize this group of people as being part of Cluster Group #2: High Income White Collar Workers. The clusters are then broken down into specifics, e.g., this group is highly mobile or most own their own homes, they volunteer and play golf. This is invaluable information to give any sponsor, not to mention in recruiting other future participants that are similar. More on this in the next chapter.

Types of Corporate Sponsorships

You are, most likely, aware of the different types of sponsorships. But for those who need a refresher course, there are three different types of sponsorships: in-kind, cash and media.

Cash

Cash is cash. Cash is always given for title, presenting and associate sponsorships (see the chart on page 162 for definitions of these sponsorship levels). We'll get into how to make the ask later.

In-Kind

An in-kind sponsorship is strictly a donation of goods or services, and it never involves any transfer of money. In-kind sponsorships are generally easier to obtain because many companies wish to provide samples of their product and/or have overages, as in the (perishable) food industry. These types of sponsorships are win-win for all. The corporation writes off the donation, provides samples of its product or service to its target market, wins loyalty and appears to be a good corporate citizen in the community. In-kind sponsorships can also involve **outsourcing** — the new strategy for the '90s (and beyond). Outsourcing is when corporations perform a task that would usually be a line item in the event budget, e.g., postage. I've found it much simpler to go to a corporation and ask for them to send a 10,000-piece mailing first class than ask for the equivalent $3,200 in a cash sponsorship. Write up a list of line items that a corporation can do for you, ones that will not compromise your timeline. Obviously, if a corporation cannot get a critical mailing out on time, it's not worth it. There are many things, however, a corporation may be willing to do. For instance, local trucking companies may be willing to pick up fruit if they usually stop at the market anyway. Ask the vendors who supply your organization who *their* trucking companies are. Don't mention the word outsourcing, simply ask them if they would mind picking up your fruit and delivering it since they're already at the market.

Some in-kind sponsorships can be quite lucrative. Recently, Universal Outdoor Midwest, Inc., in Chicago, donated *100* billboards to La Rabida Children's Hospital. I asked Mark Hirtzer, director of development, why. He replied,

> We have 4,000 billboards in the area and often we have signs that haven't been sold for one reason or another — often in great locations. In that case, we're happy to donate the signs to a charity to help deliver its message. It enhances our image in the community and helps charities reduce costs and increase revenue.

(Expect to pay for the design and production of any donated space. Regardless, it's a great deal and worth the investment. More on using outdoor advertising for recruitment in Chapter 11.)

There is another type of in-kind sponsorship — media sponsorship — which certainly warrants its own category.

Media

Media sponsorships are critical. They are often forgotten. Many of us don't try to get them because our perception is that we cannot obtain them without "knowing someone." Or, if we do, we turn in a "mom and pop-esque" proposal. I've been fortunate to have fallen into some fabulous media partnerships. In fact, the two most valuable sponsorships came directly out of my naiveté! Pick up that phone! Make a contact. Then send a formal proposal. There are no rules (except to be professional and not to get defensive if your proposal is rejected. I've been called back many times when a different department has a better fit for a project).

Walking and cycling events are particularly good promotions for media sponsors because they cost them almost nothing. Sponsors have the opportunity to air the spots when they do not have any paid advertisement. Plus, they are performing a community service and meeting FCC requirements for PSAs. Ideally, however, you'll want promotional spots *and* PSAs (PSAs are public service announcements). Be wary, however, because FCC requirements are relaxing, making it more difficult for charities, as there are fewer PSAs being offered. We'll talk in greater depth about media advertising for recruitment in Chapter 11.

An event is a great way for the station's DJ or anchor to increase his or her own marketability by acting as a chair or MC for the event. Further, it's a wonderful way for a station to showcase a new on-air personality. But don't forget that "behind-the-scenes" guy or gal: the news director, press manager or station manager. These people are definitely worth spending some time cultivating. They're often overlooked, as most charities immediately go after the on-air celebs who, quite frankly, have less decision-making authority than any behind-the-scenes manager.

I obtained one media sponsorship through the evaluation form (see Exhibit 6.2) given to every walker at the end of a walk in the "goody bag" (of sponsor coupons, samples, etc.). This "goody bag" always includes a "finish" or "completion" kit — instructions on how to pay pledges and collect prizes. (I talk more about this in Chapter 6.) This completion kit should *always* contain an evaluation form. The evaluation form "asks" the participant if he or she is interested in volunteering for a committee for the following year.

A few years back I hit the jackpot: a participant "volunteered" to be on the next walk committee. His name was (and still is) Barry Keefe, News Director of WTMX-FM in Chicago, a very popular station that eerily matched our walker demographics (female over 30). Not only did Barry secure a sizable media sponsorship at his station, which has increased its participation over the past six years, but he has increased his own personal involvement as well. Further, the station became involved in many other campaigns within the organization.

Another media sponsorship started out as a small favor . . . WLS-TV, the ABC affiliate in Chicago, agreed to play a few spots before a walking event. The station *asked* if they could send an anchor to the event to MC. The anchor the station sent was so impressed that she asked to become more involved and is now an active board member.

Never assume a TV or radio station will say no. There are a number of reasons for them to say yes — often they are looking to associate a new personality with a charity or cause to help introduce this person into the community. Another Chicago TV station, WBBM-TV (the CBS affiliate), sponsored an event by providing ten, 30-second spots for a one-day cycling event. After their initial involvement they *offered* to produce a half-hour television show and aired it twice. Why? Because the demographics of the event closely matched a market they were trying to attract to their station.

The way to target a media sponsor is to look for a station that appeals to your primary market. In the case of walking events, this market is *primarily* females over 30. (Bike tours, by the way, are typically 60% male, but this statistic is rapidly changing because in 1995 women purchased over 52% of all new bicycles.)

Typical benefits to media sponsors include:

- Inclusion of logo in/on front of brochure
- Logo inclusion on t-shirt
- Opportunity to display their signs
- Opportunity to advertise their sponsorship of your event
- Mentions in all press releases and collateral materials
- Opportunity to MC the event with on-air personalities
- Opportunity to create give-away contest, which helps to promote the event

What to ask of media sponsors:

- Production of one promotional spot
- Six to eight promotional spots per day for six to eight weeks
- Help assist in corporate team recruitment
- Assignment of personality to event
- Participation of station/personality in all pre-event promotions (parties, etc.)

- Opportunity to "back-sell" your event to clients of their station
- Opportunity to create a station corporate team

Some industry tips:

- It is much easier to get one station to be the official sponsor with a guaranteed number of exposures. A consistent delivery of one message is more effective than several different ones. It is also less expensive for the sponsoring station to produce one message.
- Send a general PSA to many stations. They will play it as long as it does not mention the other "official" station or its personalities.
- Don't expect or count on promotional spots to help in recruitment. As in outdoor advertising, it has been my experience that on-air spots help the most with retaining pre-registered participants, not necessarily recruiting new ones.
- Use the media to encourage people to sponsor the walk, not necessarily to participate themselves.

For more media and PR tips, see Chapter 11.

Meeting the Needs of the Corporate Sponsors

Corporate sponsors participate for different reasons. More than ever, corporations are giving — with an *expectation* of getting something back. This trend toward self-interest is no passing fad. A recent *Business Week* article used the phrase "strategic philanthropy."

After years of loose purse strings and little to no follow-up, corporations are looking toward that bottom line. They're putting a premium on performance and measuring how nonprofits use their dollars. And rather than seeking to just do good, companies are linking gifts to marketing campaigns. Sports gear maker Nike, Inc., is sponsoring sports events at local Boys and Girls Clubs — and then showcasing them in their national ads.*

Of course, some of our best corporate sponsorships come through because the person asking is in some way tied to who's being asked, e.g., the wife of the president of a cookie manufacturer is on your board. These are the simplest sponsorships to obtain if you "work" your board and committee right. Give your board and/or committee all the tools they'll need to do this. In fact, ask them for their contacts and write the letter for them. More often than not, however, you'll be knocking on doors and cultivating your own sponsors. This type of sponsorship is better in the long run anyway. Because if that president loses his job, you may have to kiss that sponsorship good-bye.

Most partnerships allow corporations to do the following:

- Display good corporate citizenship
- Provide samples of its product or service
- Heighten awareness

Here's a real life example of how an event can *meet the sponsors' needs.* This is a quote from Sandy Lambrechts of Nike, Inc., regarding Nike's participation as a sponsor in Mayor Daley's 3-on-3 Holiday Hoops Basketball Tournament. I think you'll find the benefits of sponsorship that Sandy mentions insightful:

- *The event absolutely targeted our basketball end-user.* Our presence reinforced Nike's commitment to, and association with, basketball. There was not a "disconnect" between the participant and the sponsor(s) as there can be in so many sponsored events.
- *The limited number of sponsors was a key element of the program to us.* This small pool of sponsors was even more attractive as each had a good fit with each other *and* with the event.

---

*Nelson Schwartz and Tim Smart, *Business Week,* August 28, 1995, p. 85.

- *Nike usually doesn't provide our product as a prize,* but this event offered the opportunity to put the latest Nike basketball footwear on the grassroots opinion leaders who are playing the game everyday. *This was extremely valuable to us.*

Sponsorship Levels

Title: "The Kellogg XYZ Walk"; start/finish banner; display banners; logo on poster, front of t-shirt, mailings

Presenting: "Kellogg Presents the XYZ Walk"; start/finish banner; display banners, logo on poster, arm or back of t-shirts and all mailings

Associate: Place logo on front bottom of brochure cover, back of poster, t-shirt back, all mailings

Product: Place logo on inside of brochure, on posters, back of t-shirts (for over a predetermined sponsorship amount. I suggest $2,000)

Special Thanks: Give a printed "credit," but do not include logo in brochure or any collateral materials.

Obviously, sponsors who donate $3,000 should be recognized differently than ones who donate $30,000. And companies who provide cash should be recognized differently than ones who provide in-kind products or services. Regardless of the size of your individual market, the perceived value of some materials is higher than others and therefore materials with a high perceived value should not be given away. These include placement of the logo on the t-shirt and on the banners.

There are always new ways to recognize a sponsor. Let's say you get a late-entry sponsorship and the brochure has already gone to print. This sponsor promises a $25,000 cash sponsorship if you can come up with a way to give the company exposure, especially through the placement of the logo. Look to corporate America for answers — they are the pros. For example, Discover Card sponsored the CMA Awards (Country Music Awards) in 1995. However, they were limited as to where they could put their logo. Signs at the concert were forbidden. Discover Card created a special temporary tattoo of the logo for all attendees who wanted to wear it. Everyone was thrilled — the audience loved them and the sponsor, Discover Card, loved it because over 100,000 people wore their logo! Think corporate! Think of ways to "chisel out" specific pieces of the event for the sponsor to "own," e.g., a rest stop. Be creative. I've even seen a sponsored port-a-pottie (yes, really! There were even signs on the inside door of the "pottie" so each person using the "facility" could not help but see their logo)!

I recommend setting an arbitrary dollar amount for population bases over one million and under one million. For instance, a city the size of New York should not *sell* their top sponsorships for less than $10,000. A city the size of Fort Worth, Texas (less than one million), however, should not sell their top sponsorships for less than $5,000. You know your market best. I am continually surprised to learn of relatively small (300 people) walks garnering thousands in sponsorship dollars. Never underestimate your product. Setting the sponsorship level is a tool for negotiation. Prices are subjective and ultimately come down to the *perceived value.*

Sponsorship Tactics, Language and Definitions

Too often in our nonprofit world we don't get our fair share of the sponsorship dollar because we simply don't know the "lingo." We can deliver the goods, but we don't know how to package them — we don't know how to prepare a sponsorship contract. Four sponsorship "buzz words" come to mind when I think of corporate sponsorships. They are: **topspin, exclusivity, back-sell** and **first right of refusal.** Once you have a solid understanding of these concepts, you'll have a good working knowledge of corporate sponsorships. Then I'll share some tips on preparing sponsorship proposals/contracts, including two good examples, one from the profit world, one from a walking event.

Topspin

"Topspin" is when one expands a sponsor's involvement in an event. This enhancement increases the sponsor's visibility to the community. It is our responsibility to help our sponsors gain the fullest promotional value for their buck. To foster topspin, we should give our sponsors creative ideas for how they can promote the sponsorship. Often we are so excited when we acquire a new sponsor we are fearful that we have asked too much. By offering additional ways for them to promote the partnership, we are helping them maximize their investment. Here are a few topspin ideas — I'm certain you'll have more of your own:

- Sponsors to tag all media for 10 to 12 weeks with the cause's logo, e.g., "XYZ corporation proudly supports JKL Charity."
- Arrange for cross-promotions on-air between sponsors, e.g., "If you sign up for the walk before June 11th at any Workout World, you'll receive a coupon for a 25% discount on walking shoes at Tom's Shoes."
- Encourage sponsors to set up internal teams for volunteering and walking (fund raising). The corporations may get additional media coverage through this as well. Sponsors should offer special hats, t-shirts, etc., to promote their company's logo/image. Get sponsors' PR departments involved through internal (employee) and external (customer) newsletters.

Exclusivity

Exclusivity is to offer a sponsor the opportunity to be the only sponsor in a specific product or service category. For instance: If Coca-Cola is an exclusive sponsor of an event, other soft drink brands (and possibly other beverages) would not be served.

First Right of Refusal

First right of refusal is offering the sponsor (typically the exclusive sponsor) of an event the opportunity to be the first sponsor asked the following year. The sponsor has the "first right" to refuse before you can go to any other sponsors. The flaw: A new potential sponsor may come onto the scene and offer a lot more in cash and in-kind, but you are already committed to asking the former sponsor because of your agreement.

Back-Selling

Back-selling is most often used in media sponsorships, but it can be applied to many other areas of sponsorships. In a "back-sell" your media sponsor will "piggy-back" with his or her clients and effectively "sell" your event to them. This is not automatic — you must *ask* for it. Some savvy media managers will already be thinking of how they can get their clients involved, especially if it is good fit for them (e.g., a natural spring water company may want to sponsor a rest stop with a radio station or a shoe manufacturer may want to "tag" their TV ads with your logo on the bottom).

Establishing a Sponsorship Strategy

In establishing a sponsorship strategy there is no fast-food formula for a sponsorship package that will work for all events and sponsors.

The following key elements should be considered and incorporated in developing the merits of your event and when positioning it in a sponsorship package.

Sponsorship HOT Buttons

- Market demographics
- Merchandising and sampling opportunities

- Association with event (Is fit right?)
  Appeal and image
- Exposure
  On-site visibility
  Radio and television
  Print (newspaper and promotional pieces)
- Cross promotional opportunities
- Event attendance and growth potential
- Ownership of the event or a particular feature within it
- Brand or category exclusivity (will there be another brand of soda?)
- Added value potential
- Dollar value of sponsorship

The best way to formulate a proposal or obtain a corporate sponsor is to start with a question that would lead to the sponsorship strategy:

What can I provide for potential sponsors as benefits to enhance their images and sales of their product or service?

Sponsors involve themselves in sporting and other special events for demographic compatibility inherent within that particular event. The following are case studies of effective integrated marketing opportunities that were positioned to corporate clients as potential sponsorship opportunities. If an appropriate event does not exist, one can be created to suit the needs of a sponsor, or existing benefits may be created and tailored to fit the objectives of a potential or returning sponsor.

The following case study was contributed by Glen Ryniewski of the Chicago Mayor's Office of Special Events.

CASE STUDY
The Taste of Chicago

The Taste of Chicago, the supreme eating extravaganza, is one of the largest events in the United States, with more than 3,000,000 people attending each year (in less than one week). In 1995 the event celebrated its fifteenth anniversary. One of the newest elements of that year's event was the creation of designated dining areas for the public (in previous years people simply ate their food while walking around).

The Mayor's Office of Special Events used these new areas as a joint sponsorship opportunity between them and one of their newest media sponsorships, WBBM (the premier news radio station in Chicago). These dining pavilions (1,600 square foot tents) could accommodate up to 150 individuals at a time.

The dining pavilions were designated as areas for which WBBM would have "sell-through rights." A sponsor would be granted "ownership" of any chosen pavilion(s) with signs and opportunities for couponing, sampling, etc. — opportunities which create awareness. WBBM was also allowed to incorporate its logo within the pavilions for additional exposure. In addition, WBBM used this **added-value** opportunity to create a **media back-sell** whereby they sell a promotional package to *its own client list*. WBBM's sales staff now had the ability to not only "sell" a client radio spots, but offer the client participation in an event that attracted 3,000,000+ people. The pavilions offered the comfort of seating and an escape from the large crowds and offered sponsors a captive audience for name and image visibility along with sales leads and couponing.

WBBM's contribution to the event (besides sponsorship dollars) was a series of radio "spots," which was broadcasted live from the event and was a driving force in the success of the Taste of Chicago.

Other Dining Pavilion Sponsors

Another dining pavilion sponsor was NYLCARE. A large NYLCARE target is senior citizens. NYLCARE provided musical acts, dancing and other senior activities, including a Senior Day, at the Taste of Chicago.

TCF Bank utilized their pavilion space to sign up individuals for free checking accounts. In 1996 TCF Bank provided cash machines, which also dispensed coupons with cash.

Best Foods capitalized on the crowds by distributing coupon books for mayonnaise, mustard and other food products. The books were distributed by a mascot dressed as a sandwich which, of course, created photo opportunities for the press.

The following are quotes from Mark Curatolo of NYLCARE and Val Carolin of WBBM-AM regarding their involvement in the Taste of Chicago. While reading, keep in mind that WBBM-AM back-sold a part of *their* sponsorship to *their* own client, NYLCARE.

Mark Curatolo:

To reach the senior market at Taste of Chicago, we needed to provide some extra seating, extra giveaways and extra reasons to pick our eating area over the several others available to Taste-goers. WBBM and the city's Office of Special Events went the "extra mile" to help us get our message out to seniors.

Cross-marketing with media giant WBBM-AM enabled us to afford the sponsorship of the Senior Oasis and get the word out that our Oasis was available to seniors. WBBM staff went all out to make our Oasis operation work and to promote it.

In the future — based on our successful first-year program — we'll expand the Oasis to include in-tent promoting, provide additional services to seniors and their families and attract many more seniors to the Taste of Chicago as a guest of the city and NYLCARE.

Val Carolin:

The partnership between the Mayor's Office of Special Events and WBBM-AM is truly unique. As far as I've been able to discover, no other relationship of this type exists in a major metropolitan market.

By working together to sell city events, we have been able to bring additional dollars to the city's door, while offering unique opportunities to our advertisers to participate in community events. This partnership allows our advertisers to display good corporate citizenship; to sample products; and to heighten awareness through promotional advertising, signage and on-site visibility, coupled with an advertising schedule on WBBM-AM.

Developing, Cultivating and Qualifying Prospects

Time and time again I see development professionals looking through top business lists, such as the Fortune 500, or going to the library to target particular food sponsors and the like. But perhaps a far more efficient (and profitable) way in which to prospect for sponsorships is to look right in your own backyard. *Here are the most overlooked, but lucrative, potential contacts for corporate sponsorship.* Perhaps they work for large corporations or know someone who does:

- Past donors
- Top fund raisers
- Clients, members or other people affiliated with your organization
- Your employees and their family members
- Retired employees
- Committee and (especially) board volunteers
- Recipients of your services
- Recommended corporations, preferably with contact names, from *current sponsors!*

After you have assembled a list of prospects which you suspect have a similar target as your event, contact each company's marketing department and ask which department handles sponsorships. Next, as Kim stated above in "Selling Your Sponsor," call contacts to determine their needs and to see if there is a fit before tailoring a proposal. The sponsorship proposal (including the cover letter and agreement) is actually one of the *last* things you will do when soliciting a sponsor.

The Sponsorship Package

My three year old nephew always cries and says seriously, "Auntie Cindy, don't say 'stupid'" when I use the word in a conversation! Forgive me, Scott, but sometimes your aunt is *"stupid."* Sometimes she writes really long, detailed proposals,

covering each and every little bitty boring detail . . . and guess
what? They were, as they say, "filed"! So, for all my development friends out there, keep it simple (and exciting, enthusiastic
and quantifiable — this will set you apart from everyone else).
But never, never be cutesy — cute does not sell! I've included key
elements from great sponsorship proposals (pages 173 to 176):
The City of Chicago's 1996 Air & Water Show Official Product
Sponsor proposal and a proposal from a made-up national health-
care organization (see Exhibits 9.1 and 9.2). While it's tempting
to skip the next part and simply fit your information into one of
these formats, don't do it. Remember, these proposals are only
samples. No two markets are the same. You'll want to tailor your
proposal for your event.

If you've done sponsorship proposals in the past and they
worked, don't change. Remember, "If it ain't broke, don't fix it."

Sponsorship Agreement Questions to Ask Yourself

- Did I include the date of the event, payment and the terms
  of the agreement?
- Did I "date" the agreement itself?
- Did I get signatures from all parties (charity executive
  director and the sponsor's *decision maker*)?
- Are we offering the sponsor product exclusivity?
- Will there be similar/conflicting sponsors of the same
  event?
- Will the sponsors receive signs? How many, when, where,
  what size?
- Will there be any print advertising? Outdoor advertising?
  Media advertising? How much, when and where?
- Who provides insurance coverage? Who bears liability for
  the event and injury to participants?
- Who has the authority to use your logo?
- What other benefits does the sponsor receive? A private
  hospitality tent at the event? Invitations to your annual
  gala? Recognition at your annual meeting?

1996 CHICAGO AIR &WATER SHOW
August 24-25

The Chicago air & Water show is the largest two day spectator event in the United States and the longest on-going show of its kind in North America.

An estimated 2,000,000 people settle on Chicago's lakefront beaches and parks to view the finest air and water teams in the country.

The event offers a corporate sponsor the opportunity to reach a mass audience via sampling, merchandising and promotional activities on the lakefront in addition to all print and electronic exposure provided in the sponsorship package.

(Exhibits 9.1 and 9.2) Your sponsorship proposal should incorporate several key elements, including target market size and benefits for the sponsor. Look at these sections from the 1996 Chicago Air & Water Show proposal and a proposal from an imaginary nonprofit, the Lupus Foundation, for format ideas. However, be sure to tailor your proposal very specifically to your event.

Chicago Air & Water Show proposal reprinted in part with permission from the City of Chicago.

1996 CHICAGO AIR & WATER SHOW
August 24-25

Official Product Sponsor
($25,000)

Benefits

Signage:
- (10) banners on site (each 3' x 10')*
- (1) Inflatable in static display area or (5) additional 3' x 10 banners

On-Site:
- (1) Merchandising Tent-20' x 20' (includes table chairs and electricity)
- Corporate hospitality tent-with (100) VIP seating **
- Sponsor mentions during show on public address system
- UPS Aircraft participation on Saturday and Sunday
- Opportunity for visibility in static dispaly area

Event Brochure:
- Corporate/Brand logo on 80,000 copies

Program Book:
- (1) Quarter page

Advertising:
- Corporate/brand logo on 50% of all print ads
- (10) :30 spots on official radio station (WBBM Newsradio 78)

Press Show: (August 22, 1996)
- Mentions in all press releases
- Sponsor press release in event press kit
- Sponsor mentions during press show
- (1) 3' x 10 banner displayed at press show

Performer and Sponsor receptio
- (10+) invitations to reception

*Sponsor expense
** Catering : sponsor expense

Table 1. Regional Breakdown

CATEGORY	PERCENTAGE
Chicago	40.25%
Suburban Chicago	38.50%
Outside Chicago Area	21.25%
Total	100%

Table 2. Gender Distribution

CATEGORY	PERCENTAGE
Male	50.25%
Female	49.75%
TOTAL	100%

Table 3. Age Distribution

CATEGORY	PERCENTAGE
18 - 24	17.17%
25 - 34	41.67%
35 - 49	32.83%
50 - 62	6.57%
Greater than 62	1.77%
TOTAL	100%

Table 4. Income Distribution

CATEGORY	PERCENTAGE
$0.00 - 20,000.00	6.30%
$21,000.00 - 40,000.00	37.01%
$41,000.00 - 80,000.00	42.78%
$81,000.00 - 100,000.00	9.97%
Greater than	3.94%
TOTAL	100%

THE 1ST ANNUAL FUN WALK SPONSORED BY THE CHICAGO CHAPTER OF THE LUPUS FOUNDATION

May 1, 1996

Event Logo

*Marketing Opportunities
presented to
XYZ Company
and
Gina Talbott*

Contact:
Kathy Event
Special Events Manager
ABC Foundation, Chicago Chapter
123 Mission Drive
Cause, Illinois 60611
312.555.1212

The Event

On Saturday, May 1, 1996, over 2,000 people in Illinois will participate in the **Fun Walk** sponsored by the Chicago Chapter of the Lupus Foundation. This is a one day, non-competitive event and will pledge over $200,000 to help fight lupus. The **Fun Walk** will be held at ten sites simultaneously in the Illinois area, including Chicago, Palatine, Oak Forest, Park Ridge, Springfield, Bloomington, Peoria, Champaign, Crystal Lake and Schaumburg. More than 150,000 brochures will be hand delivered to 10,000 distribution sites throughout Chicago, its suburbs and southern Illinois. In addition, media promotion, day-of-event activities, posters, signage, busboards and billboards represent some of the venues the chapter offers sponsors.

When you become involved with the **Fun Walk,** you join other stellar sponsoring organizations including WQRS-TV, the Handy Corporation, Sunny Company, and many others. Additionally, the Fun Walk provides many opportunities for image enhancement and community presence.

This **Fun Walk** is dedicated to our communities and the people who live in them. It is our goal to raise awareness about lupus and to help make a difference in the lives of people living with lupus and their families.

The Participant

Following is the profile of a typical **Fun Walk** participant:

- Active individual with family
- 73% women, 25–45 years of age
- 60% have an average household income of $35,000 or more, 15% have an income of $175,000 or more

The Request

As an official 1996 **Fun Walk** Sponsor, we would request that XYZ Company provide:

- A 60% discount on $75,000 in gift certificates given to participants. Each participant who qualifies for a prize will be sent a thank you letter, a one-day XYZ Company pass and his or her certificate. Please see attached brochure for example
- A cash donation of $500 and an in-kind donation of $5,000 from each participating retailer

- Company involvement and support through XYZ Company "Official Registration Centers"
- XYZ Company **Fun Walk Month,** e.g., a donation would be made to the Lupus Foundation for each new credit card opened, a sponsored public relations and advertising campaign, such as "Walk on over to your nearest XYZ Company to pick up your **Fun Walk** brochure; join the XYZ Company, and we will make a donation to the Lupus Foundation on your behalf"
- Employee involvement, e.g., XYZ Company Team ... each XYZ Company retailer forms a team and competes against other competitive retailers to raise the most funds. XYZ could give internal incentives to the Team Captains and Team Members who raise the most money (vacation days, etc.)
- Camera-ready artwork for all printed materials and t-shirts

The Benefits of Sponsorship

As an official sponsor of the 1996 **Fun Walk,** XYZ Company will receive:

- Prominent logo/name presence in prize structure
- Logo/name presence on the front cover of 150,000 brochures
- Logo/name recognition on 2,000 walker "bib numbers"
- Prominent logo inclusion on the back of 2,000 event t-shirts
- Name recognition in all PSAs and promotional materials
- Logo inclusion on five billboards, subway cards and bus advertising cards (1,500)
- Logo inclusion and article on XYZ Company in walk newsletter *Big Feat* to 2,000 registrants

Our Mission

The Chicago Chapter of the National Lupus Foundation is dedicated to the prevention, treatment and cure of lupus, and to improving the quality of life of individuals who have lupus.

Lupus Foundation Fun Walk
Contract

I hereby agree to the guidelines of this sponsorship and will carry out all of the points outlined. On behalf of my company/corporation I, the below signed, agree to sponsor the cost of the above mentioned **Fun Walk** for the above specified amount.

My company/corporation will remit the agreed-upon amount to the Lupus Foundation no later than 30 days after our receipt of the material pertinent to the agreement.

_____ _____

Gina Talbott   **Kathy Event**
XYZ Company Representative Lupus Foundation
Date _____   Date _____

If it hasn't worked, *ask the potential sponsor for his or her suggestions of form or style.* Believe it or not, it's not unusual to find sponsors (even ones making large investments) who prefer informal documentation (confirming letters). It reduces their work, is more easily understandable, and does not have to be forwarded to a legal department or outside legal counsel.

However, when dealing with a difficult sponsor or a new one, I recommend a more formal written agreement. This may sound a bit too legalese for a nonprofit. *I never advocate suing sponsors who do not meet the agreement, but the agreement heightens the parties' level of attention to their commitments prior to event day.* I might also add that I have never been let down (in any significant way) by a sponsor — except that time when our ice cream sponsor didn't show up on a 89° day!

Here are 10 specific benefits we can offer a sponsor. Please note that you will want to pay close attention — you do not want to offer all benefits to every sponsor. Reserve the most valuable benefits for your title and presenting sponsors. There's no hard and fast formula for sponsorship packages — you can tailor the following to fit your market, your potential sponsors and *their* needs. Here's the top 10:

 1. Logo inclusion on front or inside of event brochure (or flyer).

2. Logo inclusion on start/finish banner (always include exclusive media sponsors here — it validates your event).
3. Logo inclusion on front or back or arm of t-shirt (and other giveaways). A shoe store sponsor may want to give away shoelaces with its logo imprinted on them.
4. Inclusion in all pre-event promotions.
5. Opportunity to sample products and/or services.
6. Mentions in all press releases.
7. Logo inclusion and mention in all direct mail pieces to registrants.
8. Opportunity for tie-ins with other sponsoring organizations.
9. Opportunity for employee involvement.
10. Logo inclusion on all print and TV advertisements (reserve this for title and/or presenting sponsors).

Be forewarned: know your prospects' needs and don't assume anything! A soft drink company may not really care about logo inclusion anywhere, but wants the opportunity to provide samples of its product at the event. A snack food company may be interested in your event because women purchase its product, but they aren't the largest consumers. A few years back I "assumed" that Hostess Cupcakes would not be a good prospect for a long-distance bike tour. "After all," I thought to myself, "Hostess caters to moms who buy snack food for their kids." WRONG. Hostess' largest market, it turned out, was men between the ages of 18 and 29 (a near exact match to our bike tour participants). *Research your prospects!*

Sponsorship Resources

The best sponsorship resources are through IEG, Inc. (International Events Group), out of Chicago, Illinois. This is not a commercial or paid endorsement. IEG is simply the premier provider of quality information on sponsorship. Perhaps you already subscribe to the *IEG Sponsorship Report*. The report presents profitable ideas that work across a broad spectrum of sponsorships, including causes. They provide contact names and telephone numbers of all decision makers who are featured in the reports. In addition, IEG publishes the *Guide to Sponsorship,* the *Sponsorship Sourcebook,* and the *Legal Guide to Sponsorship* as well as a workshop series. IEG's address and telephone number are listed in the back of this book under Resources.

Sponsorship Follow-up and Acknowledgments

Although Chapter 7 has sections on acknowledgments and recognition, sponsorship warrants its own space. As I'm sure you've experienced in other campaigns, an unrecognized sponsor is a sponsor no more. Just like past participants are the best fund raisers, past (satisfied) sponsors increase their involvement and commitment every year.

It sounds too simple — a thank you. Unfortunately, as we've all experienced, the day after an event is over, our focus often shifts right into the next event and the acknowledgment is sent too late (or never sent). A common thought is, "Scott over at Acme really likes me and we're 'friends' — he won't mind if I thank him later — he will understand." This is the type of thinking through which sponsorships are lost. First of all, Scott may not need that letter, but his home office or boss might.

I'm talking specifically about a thank you letter here, but what I really should call it is a sponsorship acknowledgment package. This package should contain the following:

- A *personalized* thank you letter to all involved within a corporation
- A copy of all materials in which their logo/image appeared (press clippings, location of billboards and the number of promotional spots on TV)
- Sample t-shirts (if their logo appeared)
- Invitations to event recognition party (where they will be recognized). (If you're not having a thank you party for volunteers and top fund raisers, invite them to your annual meeting and present a plaque to each person you wish to thank.)
- Statistics on walkers and volunteers
- How much *their* corporate team raised (if applicable)

- Number of sponsor products sampled (if applicable)
- An invitation to be acknowledged at the next board meeting (with senior-level leadership)
- A copy of the follow-up newsletter, highlighting the sponsor's involvement
- The sponsor post event report (see Exhibit 9.3). Include a postage-paid envelope!

Sponsor Post Event Report

Event _____ Event Date _____ Report Date _____

Market _____ Reported by _____ Company Name _____
            (optional)   (optional)

Please rate the following on a scale of 1 to 4: 1=Poor, 2=Fair, 3=Good, 4=Excellent

Media Involved (rate based on XYZ's exposure):

Radio	1	2	3	4
TV	1	2	3	4
Print	1	2	3	4

On Site Exposure:

Booth	1	2	3	4
Signage	1	2	3	4
P.A. Announcements	1	2	3	4

Event Attendance (estimated total attendance _____)	1	2	3	4
Match with Company Demographics/Psychographics	1	2	3	4
Employee Participation	1	2	3	4

Store Involvement (if applicable)

(counter cards, banners, etc.)	1	2	3	4
Communications/Follow Through of Staff	1	2	3	4
Positive Image Association		Yes	No	
Do you plan to participate in the event again?		Yes	No	

What changes would you make to the event?

_____

_____

_____

_____

Other comments:

_____

_____

_____

_____

(Exhibit 9.3) This evaluation should be mailed to your sponsors in the acknowledgment package along with a self-addressed stamped envelope. It will be a big help when you're planning for next year.

In addition to formally thanking your sponsors, it is equally important to keep in touch with your sponsors year-round. Make what I call an "off-the-clock" call. Call when you are *not asking for something!* Simply call to say hello and ask how he or she is, how the person's family and business is, etc. You'll be amazed at how much it is appreciated.

Ten

Creating Incentives to Participate and Increase Revenue

Meeting the Needs of Your Participants

Most walkers (approximately 85%) will say they participate because it helps the cause. As I mentioned earlier in the book, I surveyed more than 1,000 participants of a walk and 85% said they participated because of the cause. Yet, when given the opportunity to *donate their prize back* (except for the t-shirt), less than 3% actually did so. Prizes are important. Being recognized is important, too.

It has been my experience that people participate *and raise money* for many different reasons. What motivates people to join? What motivates them to raise more their second year? Most of all, how do we meet the needs of our participants and potential participants?

Why do people participate? Most people participate for the following reasons:

- It's fun (and a no-cost outing)
- The prizes
- To meet people
- A good cause
- To be part of something BIG
- To be noticed/to get recognized
- To feel good about helping others
- To exercise

Prizes

Let's focus on prizes for a bit. Prizes are important to participants — but only the right prizes. The prizes must be what your target wants and/or needs! If your data tells you that your participant base is white collar females who own their own homes and eat out a lot, you may want to include restaurant certificates or mail-order catalog certificates.

As a general rule, prizes should not exceed 5% to 7% of the amount raised, excluding t-shirts. However, the perceived value must be at least 15% of the amount raised. For example, if a participant raises $100, the amount spent on the prize should be between $5 and $7, with the perceived value at $15 dollars *or more*. (Naturally, it is *always* best to get prizes *donated*. But the reality is that you'd better budget for prizes; prizes are extremely hard to get donated.)

A higher perceived value can be achieved with little effort through the following ways:

- Negotiating with sponsors for prizes at cost
- Negotiating with chain restaurants, direct mail houses, etc., for a percentage off the face value. I recently negotiated with a local restaurant chain to give us 40% off the face value of certificates (to be used like cash) in exchange for their logo placed in the brochure under the prize category
- Buying close-outs directly from manufacturer
- If you have more than one pledge-based event, buy in volume to get a discount.

Structuring Prize Levels

The way in which you structure the prize levels is critical to the financial success of your walk. If you have past data, it will make this process much easier. You'll want to analyze the following data from pervious walks:

- How many walkers fell into each prize category?
- How many walkers got just to the prize level and stopped raising any more money?
- What were the most-liked prizes (you can get this information through your walker evaluation form)?
- Would participation be affected if you raised prize levels?

If you are in your first year and do not have previous data, here are some general guidelines and a sample prize structure:

- Don't make your categories too far apart at the higher levels or people will stop raising funds when they achieve a prize category. For example, if you have a $500 category, it is tempting to make the next category $1,000 (an even number). But a better choice might be $750, as it is more attainable and people will be less likely to stop raising money after $500 if they feel they must raise $500 more to get to the next prize level.
- Make the initial prize level *easy* for most people. If registrants feel they can easily achieve the first category, they'll be more likely to feel inspired to do more.
- Never think your participants are greedy. It's a game. Everyone wants to get the most possible for the least amount of effort. It's human nature.
- Never make your prize structure cumulative. Some colleagues disagree with me, but I believe the only way to give something of value is to offer only premium products with good brand names. If your prizes are cumulative, your only alternative is to offer junk (unless you're willing to blow your profit margin and go way over budget). In addition, giving out cumulative prizes are a nightmare and cost a lot more in postage or UPS fees.

- Research competitive walking events and see what they give. Make your prizes more alluring.
- Participants prefer items with a logo. Consider corporate sponsor logos as well as your event logo (it's free advertising every time they wear/use it!).
- *Always* have two selections for each prize level.

Prize Structure

$5,000 TV and VCR *or* $500 of The Electronic Store Certificates

$3,500 Luggage Set *or* $350 of The Electronic Store Certificates

$2,500 Sony Stereo *or* $250 of American Airline Certificates

$1,700 Private Party for 25 *or* $170 of Dinner Certificates

$750 Sony Cassette Clock Radio with Speakers *or* $75 of Certificates

$500 Six-month membership to a health club *or* $50 J.C. Penney Gift Certificates

$300 *Oversized* Walk logo Umbrella *or* $30 of Chili's Certificates

$200 Walk Gym Bag *or* $20 of Gift Certificates

$125 Official 199__ Walk Sweatshirt

$75 Official 199__ Walk T-shirt

A minimum of $25.00 per walker is required to participate.

PLACE INCENTIVE FOR TOP FUND RAISERS HERE . . .
such as a special drawing, e.g., all walkers who turn in more than $500 on walk day will be entered into a special drawing for a trip, etc.

Note: This will also encourage people to bring their money with them on walk day!

Some "out-of-the-box" (unusual) prize categories:

- Advertise in your brochure that all participants raising over $200 will have the opportunity to win a trip (donated, of course!).
- In your newsletter, advertise that the corporate teams averaging more than $175 for each member will be invited to a *private* event party.
- Advertise that all participants who raise more than X amount will have the opportunity to appear in the local

newspaper or in a radio show (pre-arranged with your media sponsor).

As you can see, there are a number of different ways in which to specifically increase the pledge amounts of registrants before event day. I'm certain you'll have many more ideas of your own.

Attracting Corporate Partners as Prize Sponsors

As I stated above, it is very difficult to get prizes donated. However, I have to qualify that statement. If you have sponsors on board who often use their logo on merchandise, such as Nike, the kings of logo placement, ask them to sponsor a prize category. They may even be looking for opportunities. But be sure to *ask* — they may not even think of it. Merchandise is always off-site in a warehouse distribution center — they may even be willing to send out the prizes from their warehouse.

Prize Fulfillment

Prize fulfillment is the process whereby you distribute the prizes. Just as it is important to acknowledge your sponsors, it is equally or more important to acknowledge your participants. Once they have turned in their money, they expect their prizes. Tell your participants (on the prize form in the "completion kit" handed out on event day) how long it will take until they receive their prizes. I recommend getting prizes to the participants within six weeks from the date they turn their pledges in. The easiest and least expensive way to fulfill gifts on time is by not having to send a physical gift. What I mean by that is to incorporate gift certificates into your prize structure as much as possible. People not only like certificates because they can choose exactly what they want, but it costs only $.32 to mail the envelope (as opposed to $3 to $8 for one prize)!

Even if you incorporate certificates, you'll most likely have to do quite a bit of mailing. Here are the most popular choices for fulfillment:

A fulfillment house. These people know prize fulfillment better than anyone. It's expensive, but if you calculate the true cost you will incur, it might not be out of reach. Many premium incentive companies offer this service, but be wary — they'll often tag a sizable additional amount for handling. Negotiate!

In-house. In-house means just that — using your employees, your time, good record keeping and distribution systems.

And then there is thievery. I've always kept prizes on hand and kept what I felt were adequate inventory controls. I'm continually amazed at the amount of "mortality." In addition, there are space constraints, which many nonprofits face, as well as time constraints. I've done it both ways, and the fulfillment house is the way to go. If you plan on attempting this in-house, be forewarned of potential costs and problems. Hidden costs may include staff time for packaging, handling returns, and dealing with angry participants. You may lose a lot of future participants if this process is not done correctly. At least in the case of the fulfillment house, people can call them and complain and it is not associated with your organization as much as it would be if you were handling the mailings in-house.

A national department store. Many department stores have premium or special market divisions, often called corporate incentives or premiums. Department stores receive sizable discounts on UPS and can often pass on that savings to your organization. Consider using gift certificates from these stores in your prize structure.

At the walk. If you are extremely organized and have some past data as to how many of your walkers turn in money on event day, you can attempt to do this. Again, it is a logistical challenge. Further, you must estimate well before event day as to how many prizes you'll need. Prizes are usually not returnable. So if you over-order or place the wrong order, you're stuck. Further, there is now a security issue of how to keep the products safe. (Although I always recommend handing out t-shirts on event day to people who turn in the minimum amount to get a t-shirt — usually over $50.) Not only do people want to wear them on event day, but it *significantly* reduces mailing costs and the time involved to send them out later. Further, it creates an incentive itself to turn in pledges on event day!

Increasing Revenue

There are many low-cost or no-cost ways to increase revenue. The main ways in which to increase revenue are through more new participants, more repeat or past participants, more sponsors per participant and higher pledges per participant. Incentives help create "brand loyalty" and increase pledge averages.

The most effective and least expensive way to lure individuals into raising more is to recognize them. One way to recognize walkers is to create special name tags, ribbons, shoelaces or buttons for special categories such as top fund raisers or veteran walkers. Remember, the cost must be low! Believe it or not, walkers love a simple ribbon they can wear on event day. Be sure to come up with a catchy and creative name for each individual club (see Chapter 5, on page 51 for tips on name creation). It's a great conversation opener and makes the event more festive. Another way to increase revenue is to increase walk sites (create new routes). More about site expansion later on in this chapter.

Here are a few of my favorite clubs and sample incentives:

Special Clubs and Recognition

For past participants or "veterans" (Heart & Sole Club)
For top fund raisers over $500 (Bronze Toe Club)
For top fund raisers over $1,000 (Silver Toe Club)
For top fund raisers over $5,000 (Elite Feat Club)

Whatever incentive you choose to distribute for each category, it must be given out on event day (at registration). In fact, you may even want to set up speed registration for certain club members as an additional incentive. Create new incentives for each category, e.g., offer valet parking for all $1,000 fund raisers or "Quick 'n' Easy Registration" for all top fund raisers. The ideas are limitless. Find out what your participants want! One warning though: If you advertise these incentives, make sure you can come through. It is imperative that the incentive be handed out on event day. People will become very disappointed if you run out — these recognition incentives mean a lot.

A great incentive that costs only 25 cents or so is to have a special logo printed on the t-shirts for veterans and team members. Be careful not to get too crazy by giving a special insignia for each and every little special club you create. Limit the special insignias on t-shirts to only those who raised over $500 or those who are veteran walkers. (I always used a gold star saying "Walk Veteran" or "Frequent Miler"). I'm certain you'll come up with some really catchy names. I must warn you, however, it can be a logistical nightmare on registration day if you are not prepared and do not have adequate, trained volunteers in place.

Turning the $60 Donor into the $100 Donor

Although our walk participants are not actually donors (because they are soliciting from others), the fact remains, how do we get these individuals to do more? It is our responsibility to educate these donors as to how they can raise more money. Some donors, however, will never raise more than the required amount just to qualify for a t-shirt. But most, given the opportunity, will raise more money.

Educate, educate, educate. In all communication pieces (especially in the newsletters and brochures) there should be tips on how to raise more pledges.

Here are a couple of simple tips on increasing revenue:

- Tell registrants to ask the company they work for to "match" their pledges. Many organizations already have matching gift programs as part of their community affairs or human resources department. However, many organizations don't — but that does not mean that their companies will not match their funds. (Some companies match funds two or three times the pledged amount.) *It is important to include a matching gift list of all companies known to have matching gift programs in your area!* (See matching gift card, Exhibit 10.1).
- Always reprint your prize structure in all newsletters. Often, participants lose their brochure and/or forget to

Would you like to double or even triple
your gift to the
(your charity's name here)

...without doing any extra work?

—and—

Win a higher level prize?

here's how...

CNA INSURANCE COS. CONSOLIDATED PATERS INS. CONTINENTAL GROUP DIGITAL EQUIPMENT CORP. DUTY FREE SHOPPERS GROUP ENRON CORP. EQUITABLE LIFE ASSURANCE FIELD ENTERPRISES INC THE FIELD CORP. FIRST BANK SYSTEM INC. GATX CORP. GENERAL CINEMA CORP. KEMPER GROUP KENNAMETAL INC. KIDDER PEABODY & CO. INC. ENRON CORP. EQUITABLE LIFE ASSURANCE FIELD ENTERPRISES INC	Do you or one of your sponsors work for one of these companies? These companies, as well as many others not included in this list, may match your donation or your sponsors' donation. Some will even triple the amount of your pledge! Corporate matching gifts programs provide a means of making your donations really grow. Please take the time to ask your company's personnel or employee relations department for a matching gift form. Be sure to ask if we qualify. Complete the employee portion and mail the entire form to us. That's all there is to it! **Thank you for joining the fight against (your cause here)**

(Exhibit 10.1) This matching gift card shows your participants how they can increase their contribution to your cause with minimal effort. You can include this card in your registration kit.

The list of companies with matching gift programs is for example only; there are hundreds more. Be sure to call smaller companies in your market to ask if they will offer matching gifts for your event.

open it until event day. Showcase a higher-level prize like a trip or a particularly impressive electronic item.

Site Expansion

As David Letterman always says: "Ladies and gentlemen, don't try this at home!" Multi-site routes are not for the timid and *never* for the first year! I repeat: *do not try to do more than one route your first year.*

Once you have *successfully* completed the first year, you're now ready to move onto the "next level" — multi-site planning.

What do you need to ask yourself? The first question should not be how, but where is the route going to be located. Remember, our organizations are **money driven.** Obviously, the more conveniently located the sites are, the more people there are to recruit — although I certainly do not advocate adding new sites if you are in a rural farm area and you had difficulty with recruitment the last time around with a single site. Again, *don't let logistics drive recruitment!* It does not matter that you can't possibly think of how you are going to get the rest stop food delivered to a second site; remember, logistics always work out if you plan (using a detailed timeline).

So, back to the question of *where do we put a new site?*

Here are the key indicators of a successful secondary route:

1. What neighboring city, town or village has the highest per capita income (that is also at least a 30-minute car ride away)?

2. What neighboring city has the highest density of population? Is there a McDonald's? (Yes, really. A McDonald's is often a strong indicator of population density.) To match your market more closely, look for, perhaps, a national chain like the Cosmetic Center. Since we already know more women than men walk, we want to look for businesses that cater to women. For cycling events, include places men frequent (e.g., electronic stores, auto dealers, barber shops, etc.).

I strongly recommend calling your city, town or village's Department of Planning and/or Economic Development. These departments have the most amazing resources, including lists of employers, financial institutions and service organizations.

After you get a list of cities (it may be only one if you are in a rural area), you must then ask yourself the following questions to further your investigation:

- Of those cities, which one(s) have conveniently located *and* attractive routes?

- What volunteer support network are we likely to get in that area?
- How many, if any, corporations are in or around the area? And what is the likelihood of those corporations joining our cause? And, the most important question:
- *Is there competition?* (And, who are they? What size are they? What time of the year are they planning their event?) When I say competition, I do not necessarily mean the exact same type of event. If you are doing a walking event, an established cycling event could recruit many of your prospective participants. And, especially in smaller communities, there are only so many resources to go around. I'm always for trying, regardless of the competition — just be sure you've done your homework. Most of all, know *when* they are doing their event. In larger markets it is especially tough to do a competitive analysis. One of the easiest ways to determine who is doing events is by contacting the permit office of your park district and asking who has what dates reserved. The MS walk nearly always takes place just three short weeks before the mother of all walks, the March of Dimes Campaign for Healthier Babies, and both are still growing strong despite tough competition for the same dollars.

Once you have determined your next site and you have — again — completed a successful year (and your revenue has increased at least by 5%) you can now look to add another route using the same process.

Setting Up a Command Center for Regional or National Expansion

If you are based in the national office of a nonprofit, you may be considering setting up a regional or national department specifically designed for a walk, or whatever sporting event you are producing. Call this department whatever you wish, but for our purposes here, I have named this department the *Command Center*, basically an in-house consultant. A regional or national

Command Center will not only save significant amounts of money through volume discounts, but it can also relieve staff of gritty details (from choosing colors for the brochure to getting bids on t-shirts), freeing them to concentrate on recruitment and logistics. A Command Center will significantly help the smaller chapters out there; in the past, they could only dream about holding this type of event. Further, this buying power often helps chapters in rural areas compete and even surpass other local charities because their image has been enhanced by the national buying power. The Command Center also acts as a clearing house, disseminating information from other offices which is often not shared (direct mail pieces, recruitment ideas, etc.). As I stated in the beginning, *don't reinvent the wheel!* These Command Centers can be set up to do as much as you want them to. But before investing time and effort in this major undertaking, poll your constituents, your executive directors from participating chapters or offices. Some chapters may consider it a control move by a national or regional office; others (the smart ones) will see it as an amazing opportunity to do "big-time" events.

Command Centers can also significantly help package the mission and image of the nonprofit through a coordinated effort. If local offices are left with coming up with a name, designing the brochure and so on, the event may never take off because of budget constraints, time constraints, etc.

The reason I bring up the Command Center in the logistics chapter is because, in my opinion, it is the only way to develop multiple sites in a cost-efficient manner. Sure, a local chapter of a nonprofit can increase sites without having a Command Center to guide it, but the cost ratio (cost versus expenses) will, most likely, be too high (in excess of 25%).

Now, let's talk about expansion. Naturally, strategic and marketing plans and a timeline must be devised (see Chapter 3). One person must take sole responsibility for the management of this undertaking — let's call this person the walk consultant. Depending on the size of your budget and/or staff commitment, this may be a newly created position. Ostensibly, however, every department is involved (from systems to risk management) in the expansion. The following must be part of this new department for successful expansion:

- Training and development
- Materials development
  - Brochure development and design (local chapters should have an option, however, as to whether or not they use the selected or approved printer)
  - Other collateral materials which can be purchased for groups (t-shirts, hats, etc.)
- Systems
  - Investigate and purchase software
  - Training
- Public relations
  - Write "stock" press releases
  - Place all general releases both nationally and locally
  - Write all copy for promo materials
  - Secure celebrity endorsements for PSAs, local appearances
- Educational integration
  - Provide updates to staff on cause, mission and ways to integrate/tie the cause to the event
  - Aid chapters with integration of education of cause to event

As you can see, there are a number of different low- or no-cost ways to increase revenue. I'm sure you've thought of a few of your own. The more low-cost incentives, the more dollars. But remember, the incentives must have an intrinsic value — it makes participants feel better as people and more important. These all add up to financial success.

Eleven

Catching Your Target Market's Eye: Recruitment, Promotion and Public Relations

Recruitment

Recruitment of participants can be done in many ways. One way is not sufficient; successful recruitment encompasses a mix of strategies, including individual recruitment, direct mail, tele-recruiting, *personalized* direct mail, targeted direct mail, leafleting/FSIs (free standing promotions) and street distribution. Recruitment strategies change significantly as the event matures in the marketplace. Typically, strategies to recruit individuals work well in a new event, while incorporating strategies to market team recruitment works best in more mature events. Exhibit 11.1 analyzes the costs and benefits of different recruiting tactics. Analyzing your post-walk data will give you guidelines for future walks.

To obtain post-walk data, you must be aware of what data is important. We spoke about specific ways to capture data in Chapter 4, Creating a Budget and Computer Systems. To track data, be sure to code everything from brochures to direct mail pieces, then

Costs/Benefits of Recruitment Tactics

Method	Regis-trants	Actual Part.	Total Pledged	Pledge Average	Total Paid	Paid Average	Show Up Rate	% of Pledges Paid	Cost of Recruit-ment	Cost per Registrant
Street Distribution	550	275	$25,000	$ 90.91	$20,000	$ 72.73	55%	80%	$15,000	$54.55
Tele-recruiting	500	275	$35,000	$127.27	$28,000	$101.82	55%	80%	$ 2,500	$ 9.09
Past Participant Mailings	800	725	$65,000	$ 89.66	$70,000	$ 96.55	91%	107%	$ 5,000	$ 6.89
Daytime Soap Magazine	75	50	$ 5,000	$100	$ 5,000	$100	66%	100%	$ 2,500	$50.00
Women's Magazine List—Direct Mail	50	25	$ 2,500	$100	$ 2,500	$100	64%	100%	$ 1,500	$60.00

(Exhibit 11.1) Use this analysis of different recruiting tactics to determine which one is best for you.

analyze the cost/benefit ratio. This is illustrated in Exhibit 6.4, page 68, the direct mail analysis form. (Ways to code brochures and other direct mail "sources" are outlined in Chapter 6, Communications Development.) After you've coded a brochure or direct mail piece, you'll have a much better idea of where the participant came from. For those of you who do not have the luxury of previous data, look at Exhibit 11.2, which illustrates (approximate) percentages of recruitment sources. No matter how mature your event is (how many years it has been in existence), past participants will consistently emerge as the single largest recruitment source. As I've mentioned time and again, past participants are the least expensive to recruit and they raise more pledge dollars.

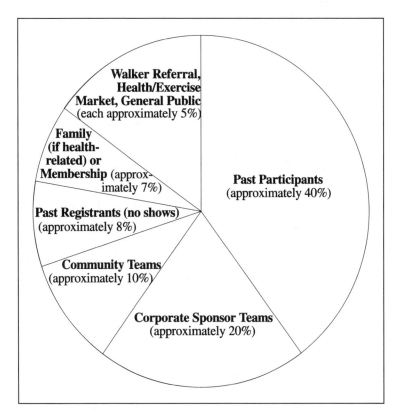

(Exhibit 11.2) Where should you look to recruit your participants? This pie chart should give you a few places to begin.

If this is your first year and you do not have data to guide you, go by the information in these charts. They are averages and you won't go wrong. And don't forget to save as much data as possible for next year's planning.

Sample Walk Recruitment Tracking Form

Source	# of Reg	Act Part	Total Pledged	Total Paid	Paid Avg.	Show up rate	Pledges Paid %	Cost*	Cost/ Person
Past Part Mailings	795	725	$62,835/$85	$64,092	$88.00	91%	102%	$4,750	$6.55

(Track as many different recruitment tactics as possible; be sure to include street distribution, direct mail and tele-recruiting.)

* Cost = cost of brochures, temporary staff, mailing house, paper and envelopes, production costs (artwork), list costs and telemarketers.

Recruiting Strategies

Individual Recruitment Strategies

One on one recruitment occurs when staff and/or board members personally recruit individual participants to the walk. This takes a lot of time and discipline and should only be done in the case of recruiting critical leadership and/or corporate sponsor teams. Individual recruitment takes a significant amount of time, so begin early . . . well before you implement other recruitment strategies. Otherwise, individual walk recruitment should be limited to strategies to recruit the masses (it's a bigger bang for your buck).

Targets for Individual Recruitment: Team captains, cause "family and friends" and corporate sponsor teams

Targeted Direct Mail

Targeted direct mail is one of the best ways to recruit participants if you already know who your audience is. You'll want to include a somewhat tailored letter and a simple way for the person to register (usually by including a self-addressed, self-stamped tear-off card they can simply fill out and drop in the mail). If you have brochures printed, send two or three along with the mailing and ask the recipients to recruit their friends. For a sample of the letter you can send to past participants, see Exhibit 11.3.

Sneak Preview Letter to Past Participants
EVENT LOGO HERE

Date

Dear **Walk for the Park** Participant:

Step into Spring! Here is your exclusive sneak preview to the greatest Walk in Illinois! Join us for the 2nd Annual **Walk for the Park,** slated for June 10, 1996.

More than ever, we need your help in the fight to keep our parks safe and clean. Help us reach our goal of 2,000 walkers and $75,000 by: registering today, recruiting a friend and organizing a Challenge Team!

Some of the highlights of this year's **Walk for the Park** include:

- Two new routes.
- Treats from Nestle, Coca-Cola, Hostess, Sunkist, Del Monte . . . and much more!
- A DETAILED map will be given out the day of the Walk marking all distances, rest stops and lunch.
- New — FAST & EASY CHECK-IN for all past participants . . . no more long lines!
- More port-a-potties, SAG vehicles and buses for all weary walkers.

Get your friends to join us in the fun! If you need more brochures, please call us at (800) 555-PARK.

Thanks for your continued support and your help in the fight for our parks!

Best regards!

Honorary Chairperson   Special Events Manager

SPONSOR LOGOS HERE

(Exhibit 11.3) Target your past participants with this letter, designed to get people excited about this year's event. After this letter, they should be checking their mailboxes every day for the registration kit!

Targets for targeted direct mail: Individuals who registered at the previous walk but never showed up, walking clubs, physically challenged participants (especially if your cause is disease or handicapped related), the family and friends of the handicapped, walking and health-related magazine lists.

Personalized Direct Mail

Personalized direct mail is the choice of the corporate giants who know the direct mail business, such as Discover Card, Mastercard, American Express, Victoria's Secret, Spiegel, L.L. Bean and many more. Personalized direct mail is much more effective than a general direct mail piece. You can not only personalize the letter by naming the individual (Dear Susan), but you can further personalize it by thanking her for raising X amount (insert her exact amount). This process is a fabulous way to recognize those special participants — those who raised the most money. Of course, this process can only be done if systems are in place which capture the data. *Plus, personalized direct mail is a great way to showcase those low- or no-cost incentives discussed earlier* (e.g., Thanks, Susan, for raising a phenomenal $283 in last year's XYZ Walk and helping thousands in Seattle. This year we're offering our top fund raisers an opportunity to register over the phone. Simply call 1-800-TOP-MONY. In addition, you'll automatically be entered in the Top Fund raiser "Golden Toe Club." In this new club you will be given special recognition in our newsletter and you'll receive a special insignia on your walk t-shirt).

Targets for Personalized Direct Mail: Past participants, top fund raisers, top team captains.

Tele-recruiting

Tele-recruiting can be extremely effective, especially when used to recruit past participants who have not registered and new registrants who are the most likely to recruit their friends to join them. I do not advocate making blind "cold calls" to people you do not know. Tele-recruiting is telemarketing, but with a single purpose in mind: Registration. Tele-recruiting is *measurable.* After X amount of calls, you'll know exactly what the calls cost, how many people were registered, and after they turn in their pledge money, you'll know how much was raised individually and collectively — only after all is said and done can you determine if the tele-recruiting was successful.

Telemarketing is relationship marketing. It is not and should not be associated with nuisance calls. It is rare to ever experience any resistance from people, especially since they know your organization. I recommend calling past participants and registrants as recruiters first.

The best tele-recruiters are your volunteers (committee members) and/or membership. If it is not possible to use volunteers, hire a reputable firm. Be wary: hiring an outside firm can be expensive and will eat into your profits. However, it is *still* cost-effective to do so, but only if you limit the calls to past participants, previous year's no-shows and registrants as recruiters. The actual cost per walker will range from $12 to $15. At an average pledge of $75 or so, it's still worth it.

When calling past participants, start calling your top fund raisers first (you'll be able to recruit about three or four walkers per hour per telemarketer). Always personalize the call by thanking them for raising X amount the previous year (see Exhibit 11.4 on page 202 for a sample of a tele-recruiting script). And it may sound obvious, but *never* call people who did not turn in pledges from the previous year.

Finally, tele-recruiters should be given a form which incorporates the following data:

- number of dials
- number of contacts
- number of yes and no responses
- reasons why people are not returning

Targets for tele-recruiting: Past participants, especially top fund raisers, new registrants, membership base, top team captains, and no-shows (past registrants who never showed up the previous year).

Recruiting to Past Participants
Who Raised over $200
(Sample Script)

Hello, (past participant's first name). My name is _____,
and I'm a volunteer for the Environmental Assistance Foundation. I'm
calling for a couple of reasons. First, I would like to thank you for participating in the 1995 **Walk for the Air,** and for raising (paid amount) —
that's quite an accomplishment! Second, I would like to invite you to participate again in our 1996 **Walk for the Air,** which is going to be held on
Sunday, June 11th. Your brochure was sent last week. Did you receive it?

If yes: Great! As a courtesy to our top fund raisers like yourself, we
            would like to offer registration by phone. Would you like to
            register today? I can take down your information in just a few
            seconds.

If no: I'll send another in the mail today. Could I have your address?

Thanks so much for your time, (first name). We hope to see you on
June 11th.

NOTE: Use volunteers or committee members whenever possible, but
            if hiring paid telemarketers, it is very important that they say
            they are volunteers.

            If you have a disease-related cause, ask "patients" to call —
            they make great tele-recruiting volunteers, and they project
            warmth and thankfulness.

(Exhibit 11.4) Here's a basic tele-recruiting script for past participants. Try to contact people during the day, rather than after
business hours. Most people don't like this kind of call after a long
day at work. Be sure to have a space for a work phone number on
the registration form, and you'll be able to use it to recruit participants the following year.

Leafleting

Leafleting is a great way to get out there and have some fun
with your event committee. Leafleting is not simply putting brochures or flyers on cars. Unless, of course, you are leafleting a
competitive event (where you go to a similar — competitive —
event and place your event brochures on cars which are parked

while the participants are out on the route). This may seem "sneaky," but it is generally accepted. If you are uncomfortable, call the other charity and ask for permission. Otherwise, stick to walking/cycling paths, other sporting events and places where you know your target will be.

Leafleting, like tele-recruiting, is targeted — and *measurable!* As discussed in Chapter 6, all brochures should be coded with a source code. Simply assign a source code, for example "B", to all leafleting brochures. Let's say you have 500 leafleting brochures and you get 50 registrants from the "B" brochures — that's a 10% return once the "B" participants turn in their pledge dollars.

Only use staff and volunteers for leafleting because it is much too difficult to put controls on hired temporary help. They can say they "leafleted" 100 brochures, but there are no witnesses. Further, staff and volunteers are the most enthusiastic and can answer questions about the specifics of your walk. Staff leafleting outings are a great way to build team play within the organization — make it a fun half day out. It also helps give staff ownership of the event.

Targets for leafleting: For walks, leaflet competitive events, places where there are women (outside grocery stores), community events, walking paths, and other in-house events (this is called cross-selling). For cycling events, also leaflet bicycle paths, sporting events (both participatory and spectator) and other venues where men gather in large groups.

Targeted Brochure Distribution

Brochure distribution ("street" or "mass" distribution as many charities call it) is, in my opinion, the most problematic of all recruitment techniques, but it is also the most successful, especially for walks that are in their infancies. Brochure distribution in and of itself is simple. Go to retail outlets and ask their permission to place your brochures on their counters in highly visible locations (often near the register). The word "targeted" is the key to successful street distribution. Brochure distributors (volunteers or paid) must be given specific instructions (through training) as to where to distribute (see list below). It is expensive, labor intensive and just plain "gritty." However, if done properly it is very rewarding. . . . as with most things in life. *Brochure distribution must be done in a timely basis, placing all brochures out in two weeks, and 12 weeks before event day!*

Distribution is costly (especially if hiring temporary distributors), but a necessity. In a newly created event, brochure distribution can account for 50% of all registrants. In a more mature event, brochure distribution may account for only 10% to 15% of registrants. Plan accordingly. This is one area you must estimate somewhat, depending on variables such as maturity of your event, your market, community, etc.

As I mentioned earlier, there are ways to manipulate data on past walkers (if you have at least one year of data) to help target your brochure distribution. Further, there are information providers like R.R. Donnelley who specialize in market penetration. *The main purpose of this data is to help you concentrate your efforts on what people are likely to participate in rather than where they live.*

How to target brochure distribution

• Get a HUGE map of your SMA (Standard Metropolitan Area).

• Prioritize zip codes — take all zip codes with the highest concentration of past participants (if you have two or more years of history, average your zip codes).

• Eliminate those zip codes which are 45 miles or farther from start.

• Calculate how many sites you will place brochures in.

For example, if you have budgeted a total of 1,000 sites (outlets), break down that number per zip code "area" (by percentage), always by the heaviest concentration of past walkers first, and assign the appropriate number of brochures (multiply 10 to 35 brochures per outlet). The number of brochures per outlet are determined by the percentage of past participants that were from the area. Place 35 brochures per outlet in areas that have the highest percentage of past participants, 10 brochures per outlet in those areas that have the lowest percentage of past participants.

• Divide all zip codes (cities) into eight geographical areas and assign distributors to each geographical territory. Make sure each distributor is given his or her street boundaries so there is no overlap.

• *Brochure distribution must be done fast: All brochures must be placed within two weeks (from the date you have started distribution) and 12 weeks before event day!*

• It is important to re-stock all your best sites (the ones in which you placed 35 brochures per outlet) approximately six weeks after initial distribution. To be safe, place pre-paid postage "re-order" cards after the last brochure or a bright yellow card with the charity name. Sometimes store owners will call, but I'm not sure it's worth the cost of printing. I recommend going to the outlets in your "best" areas in which you placed the brochures. That's the only real way to determine when re-stocking should take place. Or, if very organized, ask your distributors to write down the name and phone number of every outlet and you can make calls (this is the best way, but takes a lot of discipline on the part of distributors).

Targets for brochure distribution: Zip codes from which most participants came in the previous year's walk (if applicable) *and people who have spending habits like the people in that zip code, but may live in another zip code,* health clubs, weight loss centers, beauty shops, grocery stores, yogurt shops, gas/convenience store locations, gourmet cheese and wine shops, tanning spas, card stores, athletic footwear stores, doctor's offices (especially gynecologists' offices). Think women!

The hiring and training of distributors

Distributors can be volunteers, but I've found it exponentially more effective to use paid distributors. You must make this decision based on your budget, market size and volunteer base. Are they responsible? Are they willing to take on a large and intense project? The following are some guidelines in hiring and training brochure distributors.

Distributor Hiring Procedures

I.   **Recruitment of distributors**
   A. Call all previous distributors.
       1. Ask if they have interested friends.
       2. Encourage friends to work in pairs.
   B. A job description should be sent to all placement centers of colleges in and around your walk sites. It should be sent one month prior to the first day of distribution.
   C. Try to determine/target specific locations which need to be saturated and buy ads in local papers.
   D. Only use a temporary agency as a *last resort.*
   E. Do not use distribution companies. *The placement and positioning of the brochures is key — brochures must be placed in highly visible locations!* Distribution companies simply drop the materials off at the door.

II. **Retention**
   A. Make the distributors feel good about their jobs.
       1. Give constant encouragement.
       2. Provide them with all necessary tools to do their jobs.
       3. Tie them in with the event.

III. **Pay**
   A. $1.00 per site plus gas reimbursement. (Budget $.10 per site for gas.) The average daily distribution is approximately 50 sites. I have seen 100 by one person in six hours and I have seen distributors who have only done 25 in the same time frame.

IV. **Job requirements**
   A. Driver's license and insurance.
   B. Minimum fifty (50) brochure locations accepted per eight hour day.
   C. Method
       1. Hold group interview/training sessions.
       2. Provide all materials at end of session.

3. Distributors within 20-minute drive of office must come in twice a week to check in.

4. *All* distributors must call in every morning between 8:30 and 10:00 to report previous day's activity.

V. Training session

A. Introduction and sign-in.

B. Explanation of program/show event video if you have one already done (to help make them feel part of something big).

C. Explanation of job.

D. Explanation of pay/responsibilities.

E. Allow them to choose locations.

Make copies of detailed maps with each area's boundaries.

VI. Materials

Give them the following materials:

1. Maps
2. Brochures
3. Brochure holders
4. Tracking sheets
5. Hour sheets
6. Bag (if available)
7. Tape
8. Pen and marker
9. Letters to mall managers and store owners with charity name so the powers that be can call event manager if they have any questions about the event or about the distributors (sometimes store owners are suspicious)

Cross-Promotion Recruitment

Cross-promotion or "cross-selling" is a term used when promoting to participants from other events, campaigns, members, corporate teams, and, most of all, to sponsors. For instance, if you had a family cycling event or gala, you'll want to promote your walk to these people as well. If you have a particularly good corporate team that has a PR department, ask them if they will help publicize your event. Ask a corporate sponsor if you can "piggy-back" a walk promotion onto their company picnic or in-house party. People who have contributed and/or participated in the past are the most likely to participate in other events. If, how-ever, an event was not well received, do not waste valuable time trying to recruit these folks for another event.

Targets for cross-promotion recruitment: Internal event partici-pants, corporate team companies, and sponsor events/promotions.

Team Recruitment

Team recruitment is the key to any event's success. Without teams, you are chasing after your tail. After all, it's a lot easier to recruit 20 people with one phone call than it is to make 20 phone calls to recruit 20 individuals. Teams can be corporate, organiza-tional or just comprised of family and friends. *Corporations with matching gift programs should be targeted first.* Kemper Insur-ance, for example, matches the amount their employees raise in pledge-based charitable events. If a corporate team raises $5,500, the company will match the amount, usually with a cap. Some companies even double or triple pledges raised! Target these corporations!

With all the competition out there, how do we recruit these teams? Teams comprised of family and friends are easier to recruit because usually they will have some connection to your cause. But how do we recruit corporate teams, especially since many large corporations are already committed to the "other" chari-ties? (As you might imagine, this is the reason corporations give to avoid becoming involved.)

The March of Dimes "Walk America" walk, in my opinion, is the most successful at team recruitment. The Multiple Sclerosis "Super Cities Walk" is another. In a bit, I'll share some insider secrets on team structure and creating a timeline from the most suc-cessful charity walks. But first, here's how to recruit corporate teams.

A few good tips:
• *Find your own niche.* For example, the "Strides for Safety" walk targets kids and teens. The natural "fit" for this

organization is corporations and/or organizations that cater to kids, like the Department of Education, the Office of Highway Safety, car manufacturers and youth coalitions. Perhaps you have a disease-related cause, but most large corporations in your community walk in the Walk America walk. If this is the case, target medium-sized corporations or law firms (law firms rarely get "hit up").

• *Recruit board members' corporations and civic organizations.* Make it easy for your board members to recruit their own corporations. Give them all the tools they will need, including a pre-written memo to their employees asking for their support, a list of suggestions for internal incentives (e.g., a day off for the top fund raiser, lunch with the chair of the company, a gift certificate, etc.), and brochures and posters to distribute. The same applies when asking board members to ask their civic clubs, etc.

• *Solicit sponsors.* Sponsor teams are the best teams in my opinion, but the most often forgotten. We get so wrapped up in the logistics of the sponsorship that we often forget about our sponsors who are right there. First, if they are sponsoring your event, they are most likely not previously involved with a competitive walk. They have already taken ownership and are often eager to get more involved. (Sponsorships often come out of satisfied corporate teams!) Again, make it easy for your sponsor contact to form a team. Perhaps your contact would like to assign a different person to be the team captain. Remember, the higher up on the corporate ladder the person is, the better the response. Employees like it when they'll have "access" to the "big boss," particularly in large corporations.

• *"Scientific" prospecting.* Be serious about prospecting for teams. Develop a well thought out "prospect list." Here are the *best* sources:

- Association of Human Resources Professionals
- Association of Business Communicators (IABC)
- Past top fund raisers who work
- Chamber of Commerce list
- Committee contacts/corporations
- Walkers who identified their company on registration form
- Dun & Bradstreet
- The Harris Industrial Guide

- Yellow Pages
- Business Pages
- Minority newspaper advertisers
- Vendor lists (from your own charity *and board members*)
- Local advertisers

Exhibit 11.5 is a sample of a corporate team sign-up sheet.

---

corporate team SIGN UP SHEET

corporation name here

_____

date here

EVENT LOGO HERE

cause here

OUR GOAL IS TO RECRUIT (number) **WALKERS AND RAISE $** (dollar amount here)

team name _____ for details call team captain _____ at _____

I. _____   11. _____
2. _____   12. _____
3. _____   13. _____
4. _____   14. _____
5. _____   15. _____
6. _____   16. _____
7. _____   17. _____
8. _____   18. _____
9. _____   19. _____
10. _____   20. _____

DON'T FORGET: All team members must fill out an individual registration form and **your team name must appear on form**). All team members are responsible for raising a minimum of $50 each in pledges. Pledges are due on (date here).

For further information, contact: your team coordinator @ (telephone # here)

(Exhibit 11.5) Encourage people to form corporate teams with a simple sign-up sheet like this one.

Corporate Team Timeline

The corporate team timeline will vary from organization to organization, depending on the size of your event, your volunteer base, and time. Be sure to tailor the timeline to your event and resources.

5 Months Before
- Write tele-recruiting script
- Develop prospect lists
- Write a fact sheet to give to all team captains
- Compose sample pre-written memo so all captains can send out to potential members
- Write press release on teams
- Print all team recruitment items (to be sent to prospects)

4 Months Before
- Assemble team packets for registrants
- Recruit or hire tele-recruiters
- Research places to hold team captain training sessions

3 Months Before
- Tele-recruiting training session
- Tele-recruiting begins
- Team sub-committee to personally call all top 75 team captains from previous year
- Team information packets sent (to potential corporations)

2 Months Before
- Telemarketing to all registered team captains to motivate, encourage, and give support
- Track team registrations
- Order signs for teams (e.g., team meeting tent, team registration)
- Plan day-of-event team logistics (e.g., photos, judging of costumes, signs, registration, etc.)
- Team training session for all team captains to date

1 Month Before
- Second team training session for all new team captains

- Begin planning for team recognition party location and events
- Write a team captain "thank you" letter

Post Event

- Create a team pledge tracking form and monitor — weekly — team pledge fulfillment (ongoing)
- Mail team captain "thank you" letter the day after the event

1 Month After

- Pledges due
- Write/design and produce invitations for team recognition party

2 Months Out

- Team party

Internet Recruiting

Before I get into recruitment techniques of the internet, I would like to spend a little time talking about what the internet is and what types of information can be accessed and transmitted.

The internet is a "network of networks" originated years ago by the U.S. government. The goal was to create a computer communication system that would function even after an atomic bomb attack. As time went on, the federal government joined with universities and then large corporations to hook together a number of computers to communicate information and files. This interconnected system is called the internet.

The internet is currently growing by 90% each year — a staggering amount. While the internet is basically "free," hooking up to the internet is not. There are a number of ISPs (Internet Service Providers) at reasonable prices (usually about $60 to $100 per quarter for an individual user). Look for a provider that is based in your community (and that provides support; many are less expensive, but offer no help). This way, you are paying for a local call, yet you can interact with a computer in France!

So much can be done on the internet that entire books have been written on the subject. You can send e-mail to Israel, have a debate with someone in Uruguay, research new cancer treatments in Japan and get files from Italy. To learn how to use the internet, check with your public library. Many offer very good (free) classes. There also may be classes at your local community college.

Fortune magazine reported in October of 1995 on Procter & Gamble's foresight in registering names for potential exclusive internet addresses. It won the right to use such names as: toilet-paper.com, pimples.com, dandruff.com and badbreath.com! It's not too early to register your walk! Think of creative and interesting names! Network Solutions, Inc. in Virginia is responsible for assigning *domain* names as they are called. Their address on the internet is hostmaster@rs.internic.net or, call them the "old-fashioned way" on the telephone at 703-742-4777. Your address on the internet is called a URL (Uniform Resource Locator). No two URLs on the internet are the same.

Two of the most exciting areas for nonprofits on the internet are the **home page** or **website** and **e-mail.** E-mail can save lots on postage when doing large mailings. Be sure to place an e-mail address space on your brochures so participants can check in for the latest updates on the walk. "The home page is a place for others to visit us on the internet," states Nancy Roberts Linder. Nancy, a professional services marketing consultant with an expertise in internet marketing, recommends home pages, but cautions would-be users to create effective and useful home page material before "racing to get a home page up on the internet." Nancy, a prolific author on the internet, offers the following suggestion to all home-page creators:

Keep your material interesting, useful and updated in order to:

1) keep visitors coming back, and
2) encourage visitors to call or e-mail you when they have questions.

A home page is a great way to market events and "advertise" by posting information about your cause, upcoming events, registration forms, etc. But be wary: The codes of behavior on the internet are not to be messed with and traditional advertising will simply not be acceptable. The reception you get depends on the value of the content of your message and whether it is targeted at the right audience. If you get a negative response from someone on your e-mail list, it is important to remove that person from your list so you do not send mail to him or her again. If it happens with enough people and you keep on doing it, word will circulate and the deluge of hate mail will pour in. Luckily for us, we are in a cause-based field and all of our "advertising" is "for a good cause." At least it's generally perceived that way. But again, beware: Promoting organizations on the internet is still new territory. Remember, your potential audience does not want to be treated en masse. Which brings me to what I call **internet etiquette.** Here are a few *don'ts*:

- Unsolicited e-mail or bulk mailings, sometimes called "In Your Face" or IYF advertising.
- Postings or cross postings of announcements and messages to unrelated groups or lists.
- The network equivalent of "cold calls," in which the unsuspecting consumer gets uninvited "mail."

Before setting up on the internet, seek out a consultant to help guide you to the right internet providers and resources. It will save you a lot of time, money and aggravation. Here are a couple sources to help get you started:

- Contact Max Bar-Nahum at The ORENSOF GROUPE at 1-500-ORENSOF or at his website: http://www.orensof.com. Max is a computer and internet specialist with an amazing new internet service for nonprofits which is explained in great detail below.
- *Internet for Dummies,* John Levine, IDG Books Worldwide, 7260 Shadeland Sta., Suite 100, Indianapolis, Indiana 46256, 1996.
- *Navigating the Internet,* John Levine, SAMS Publishing, Division of Prentice Hall Computer Publishing, 201 W. 103rd Street, Indianapolis, Indiana 46290, 1994.

With the proliferation of computers at work, school and home, there are more and more people connecting to the internet. This opens up a dynamically expanding venue for nonprofit organizations. For a small set-up fee and a minimal annual connection charge, smaller nonprofits can pool together into a common internet address. This would enable anyone to scan through the home pages of hundreds or thousands of nonprofit organizations' events.

Of course there would have to be a master index grouping all subscribers by geographic location, cause, type of events, etc. A potential participant could choose an event from any number of nonprofits anywhere. The potential participant could then e-mail for more information. Past participants could get automatic e-mail information and updates. Remember, home pages should not be graphically overbearing, and mass marketing is frowned upon. Organizations abusing internet users have found their e-mail boxes filled to capacity by contra-junk-mail.

A pooled "good causes" or "charity sporting events" internet address not only allows quicker registration of participants, it saves mailing costs by electronically transporting materials to the participant. It saves printing and envelope-stuffing costs, too. It also allows staff and volunteers more time to organize and promote the event and follow up on collections. Another benefit of the internet is sophisticated encryption (secret code) technology; participants could theoretically pay any fees associated with an event (or pay pledges or make a donation) by credit card on the internet.

There are many individuals who browse the internet specifically looking for charity walks or rides, etc. Such an individual would be able to access a specific cause and/or type of event — and even sign up for several events. The opposite is also true; a casual net surfer might notice an event or cause that tweaks his or her fancy. You now have a participant or a donation from a source that you would normally not have reached.

Even though events are local, the internet is global. A common "good causes" or "charity sporting events" address could potentially bring in participants and donations from all over the world (not to mention the opportunity to educate people about your specific cause). For example, a cycling club in Holland might sign up for a bicycle tour in Virginia that they saw while surfing the net. The potential of worldwide recognition, public relations and advertising is *limitless!*

Larger nonprofits can have their own exclusive address on the internet with multiple pages broken down on a state or regional level in addition to the "good cause" or "charity sporting event" web site. This will allow them multiple exposures on the net without additional costs.

Integrating Marketing, Advertising and Public Relations

Media Advertising and Timeline

It is imperative to develop an aggressive marketing and public relations program to get the word out about your event. Getting the media involved not only helps with recruitment, but it helps increase awareness about your cause (and ties the cause to the event). Your media campaign should integrate TV, radio and print advertising — not just one or two. Press releases, TV and radio spots, PSAs, announcements and proclamations from local public officials, and, ideally, a press conference announcing the event (this works best when you have a celebrity involved) should all be part of the mix.

PR Timeline

TASK	DEADLINE
• Seek radio and TV sponsorship	6 months before
• Determine billboard needs/ sponsorship	5 to 6 months before
• Contact celebrities	6 months before
• Contact magazine-type shows	5 months before
• Plan, according to budget, advertising "buys"	3 months before
• Develop radio and TV PSAs and distribute to media	2 to 3 months before

• Send cover letter, news release and other materials (posters, videos) to local PR groups	2 to 3 months before
• Determine select civic organizations and ask for five-minute spots in their programs the month before your event	2 to 3 months before
• Begin seeking creative news stories surrounding your event. Contact appropriate reporters	2 to 3 months before
• Distribute posters and brochures	3 months before
• Research "community calendar" listings	2 months before
• Send news release on event to media	2 months before
• Prepare press kits	3 months before
• Send camera-ready ads to local papers to place *gratis* if they have space	ongoing
• Seek to appear on local morning talk shows/news	2 to 4 weeks before
• Mail press kits	3 weeks before
• Place community calendar listings	3 weeks before
• Seek to speak on radio shows during drive time	week of event
• Send photo opportunity fact sheet to assignment editors at newspapers, radio and TV stations/follow up with phone calls	week of event

Television

It has been my experience that it is much simpler to get media coverage in a small town, which makes sense. But don't let that deter you if you're in an urban area; often there are slow news days when station managers look for "filler." Of course, we don't think of our event as "filler," but they might! It is also more difficult to get air time on TV than radio, but try and try again.

Unfortunately, the FCC is de-regulating radio and its rules on the amount of time a station must donate to public interest information are being lifted, leaving less time for PSAs. Therefore, work hard at hitting up stations for *exclusive* sponsorships rather than counting on PSAs to do it all. And, with a sponsorship agreement, you're more likely to get the station to produce a "real ad" (usually with one of their on-air personalities).

For day-of coverage, call the station "assignment editor" the week before, the week of, and the day before. Make sure a press kit has been sent before calling. A press kit includes: a one-page fact sheet on the event, general information on the cause and its mission, known groups or people who are already participating, special interest stories, and often a fun walk-related item, such as shoelaces with your logo or a walk t-shirt.

The recommended promotional time pre-event for television is six weeks. The number of spots should be between two and 14, averaging five to six spots per day.

Print

Print includes local newspapers, national newspapers with local "sections," city magazines, alternative magazines (be careful), weeklies, business magazines and many more.

As with any medium, you will have a greater chance of getting a response if you ask the right person, that being the person who is most likely to write about a walk, either the health beat columnist or the women's issues columnist.

Send a press release (see Exhibit 11.6 for sample format and content).

Radio

Local radio stations look for community information to announce. Radio, like television, adds credibility to your event. It makes it something BIG. Radio is particularly helpful with retention (retaining registrants).

Radio stations, by law, are required to air PSAs daily. As I mentioned in Chapter 9, ask the station to become an exclusive sponsor. The great thing about an exclusive media sponsor is that

Sample Press Release
EVENT LOGO HERE

For Immediate Release

Contact: Chairperson's Name and Phone
Event Manager's Name and Phone

Local Youth Organizations Join National "Drive Safely"

Young People March to Raise Awareness About Highway Safety

(City, State, Date) More than 2,000 people from all over Seattle will join together on (date) for a five-mile hike (location to and from) to focus attention on the critical issues of driving safety. The event is part of a nation-wide "Drive Safely" walk.

(Describe key events, speakers, public officials/celebrities, highlights of event)

The Facts . . .
According to The National Highway Traffic Safety Administration, 39,000 Americans died in motor vehicle crashes last year. Almost half of those deaths were alcohol related. Seat belt use can prevent 50% of fatalities and serious injuries suffered during crashes. Yet, only 66% of Americans buckle up, and the numbers are even lower for people under 18. By focusing on these issues at the outset of prom and graduation season, participants in "Drive Safely" will remind their peers of the power young people have to preserve life.

People interested in joining "Drive Safely" or volunteering their support should call (contact and phone number).

(Exhibit 11.6) Plaster your market's media with press releases about your event. As details are finalized, you can update your press release periodically and send it to media contacts several times before event day.

you can still send out PSAs to other competing stations. However, only the sponsor radio station's logo will appear on walk materials.

The recommended amount of promotion time on the radio is six weeks, five to 11 "spots" per day (averaging 10 spots per day).

If you match the radio station to your market, they will be more likely to air your PSAs — and you will be more likely to recruit more participants. Ask your sponsoring station to advertise "joining their station team" on walk day. The station can promote its own participation by giving out logo-studded merchandise.

Outdoor Advertising

Outdoor advertising includes billboards, bus and subway "cards," taxi signs, pole advertising, banner advertising and bus stop advertising. Outdoor advertising is a great way to retain walkers. As discussed, about 20% of registrants do not show up on event day. Billboards do a particularly great job of retaining these walkers.

Mark Hirtzer, director of development, Universal Outdoor, Inc., states:

> Billboard advertising is the least expensive type of advertising available. It is the best way to reach the greatest number of people in a specific area. People cannot "turn off" signs or leave the room while passing a billboard as many people do when a commercial comes on. If you drive, you cannot keep from seeing the image on a billboard. Billboards are repetitious and build awareness. In addition, billboards are what TV and radio stations use to advertise themselves!

Billboard companies are very likely to donate unused billboards. They are much more willing, in my opinion, to give back to the community than any other medium (perhaps because they are hit with the most community pressure). Regardless, they usually donate the boards, but production costs are on your organization.

Recommended outdoor spots: Six to 20 billboards placed in highest recruitment areas for six weeks prior to event day.

Top 10 PR Tips from a Professional

Janet Treuhaft, President of The Touch of Treuhaft and former Director of Press Relations for CBS, recommends the following 10 PR tips:

1. Use your head — watch the channels, read the papers. For example, do not ask a single woman with no children to do a story on babies.

2. Work with community affairs to get a commitment for PSAs and promotional spots. A PSA is free and *no commercial sponsors can be mentioned or posted* (so don't promise corporate sponsors that their logo will appear on any PSAs). A promotional spot is a commercial and is logged in for a specific time and a value can be attached to it. Promotional spots are better.

3. Be prepared to give benefits (what they will receive if they sponsor your event, e.g., name and logo on t-shirt, brochure, literature, signs, etc.). Suggest giveaway items the station can hand out.

4. It's never too early to approach a station, especially for sponsorship. Give at least three to five months, but a year is not too early.

5. Suggest that the station "piggy-back" their clients into your event. For example, if a station sponsors a rest stop, perhaps their advertisers would want to provide samples of their product at the stop (water or snack food).

6. Be organized. Send typed letters, press releases with correct spelling. Do not handwrite anything!

7. Know the market. Work with the station research department to find out the demographics and psychographics of the market (are they single, families, seniors?).

8. The best strategy to get your spot run is to have specific ideas when you approach a station or newspaper, e.g., a medical breakthrough, triumph over adversity or a particularly touching story about one of your walkers.

9. Cultivate relationships with behind-the-scenes station personnel, e.g., news directors, general sales managers, community affairs managers, etc.

10. Be polite. People don't have to do this. The FCC is de-regulating radio, and stations are less obligated to participate. Be polite *and professional.* They can't do everything. If they can't help you now, they may call you later.

Incorporating Education into Advertising and Public Relations

As mentioned earlier, it's important to incorporate education into all aspects of recruitment and advertising and public relations. This event will, in many cases, be one of the largest events you will do, offering your organization unbelievable exposure. It is crucial to educate the public about your cause. It is a rare opportunity that should not be missed — regardless of the recruitment value.

In educating the public about your cause, make sure to remind them of the service your organization provides *and where the money goes*. People are more likely to give to your organization if they know the funds are used appropriately.

Pre-event Promotions and Parties

Pre-event promotions and parties help promote awareness of your cause, generate publicity and provide sponsors with additional promotional opportunities. *They are not, generally, used to recruit participants.* Here's a few ideas for pre-event promos:

- Sponsor product sampling at busy lunch venues
- Participant training sessions, led by media sponsor celebs
- Shopping mall promos (with giveaways)
- Early morning coffee and orange juice at train stations (with brochure)
- Pre-event pasta party
- Hospital fitness testing at sponsoring hospital
- Corporate team kick-offs at corporation cafeterias
- Parties honoring top fund raisers and teams

Twelve

Post-Event Evaluation and Planning for Next Year

Your event must be evaluated financially, promotionally and logistically. Below are ways in which you can effectively evaluate your event and determine its financial success.

The S.W.O.T. Analysis

In S.W.O.T. analysis everything is broken down into the following categories:

Strengths
Weaknesses
Opportunities
Threats

This analysis can be extremely beneficial when planning for the next year's event. Memories of the details fade quickly — it must be done relatively soon after the event is over, preferably within two weeks. Our tendency may be to let it wait until the dust settles, but we must force ourselves to do this analysis. Do the analysis yourself, first. Then, ask key planning committee members and staff to complete one, too. This way you'll have a broad spectrum from many different vantage points. After all, you could not be at all places at all times. Perhaps a staff member assigned to the rest stop area had a completely different experience than you did at the start/finish line.

Staff Evaluation

The staff evaluation is important, too, and incredibly helpful in future walk plans. As you have probably experienced yourself, staff are often the most critical. If your participants suffered in any way, the staff suffered 10 times more (because they had to listen). Allowing staff to air their grievances and "offer up" suggestions for next year's event accomplishes two things: It gives the staff a forum in which to share their walk day experiences and it helps planning for next year, usually for logistics.

I recommend a "secret" evaluation forum. I call it "secret" because it is a way in which people will share the most information without getting personal, e.g., Shari forgot to call the tent company, Julie was late, etc. Additionally, it makes it a lot less personal to the event manager. People who would not share information for fear of "telling" or hurting someone's feelings will openly share "suggestions."

Here are the main components of a "secret" evaluation. I'm certain you'll have some revisions of your own:

1. Have *all* staff meet two days after the walk in a large room.

2. Give each staff member three pale yellow cards, three pale blue cards, three pale pink cards and three pale green cards.

3. Assign each color to a topic or question. Staff can then write down their feelings, suggestions or comments about a particular topic or question *anonymously.* For instance, you can ask the staff to write the three best things about the walk on yellow cards or to list three registration recommendations for next year on blue cards.

4. Make sure to cover the four basic areas: Recruitment, Promotion, Logistics and Registration. Write these category

names on paper and tape them to the top of a wall that everyone can see.

5. Then collect the cards and tape them on the wall under the proper heading.

6. The good areas and the areas which need improvement will then be very clear.

Committee Evaluation

Follow above procedure for committee members as well.

Day-of Volunteer Evaluation

Every volunteer should get a volunteer evaluation form upon check-in. Ask them to fill out the evaluation there, or have pre-paid envelopes for them to mail in.

Participant Evaluation

Every participant should be given the opportunity to voice his or her opinion in a form designed for that purpose. Often, participant evaluations yield new insights as to what your market needs and/or wants. Some recommendations will be "out-of-the-water" suggestions (ridiculous), but acknowledge them anyway. While the evaluations can be anonymous, always ask for the name and address of the participant so you can respond via letter. (By the way, try not to get defensive when responding. As in many situations, the participant may be upset about something else in his or her life and be taking it out on your event.) Do, however, read the words "through the music" and revise your walk plan accordingly.

Evaluations should be measurable. Take a moment to go over the participant evaluation in Exhibit 12.1. Notice that the responses may be rated from 1 to 5. Be certain to tabulate the responses after most pledges have been turned in. Again, these tabulations should not be left until it's time for the next walk. Be proactive — plan ahead.

EVENT LOGO HERE

The (name of event) was a huge success thanks to you! Please help us make next year's event even better by completing this evaluation form. Thanks again for your support!

Check the route that you walked:

- [ ] route A   [ ] route B
- [ ] route C   [ ] route D
- [ ] route E   [ ] route F

Please evaluate these elements of our event:

	low				high
1. availability of (event) information	1	2	3	4	5
2. information in brochure	1	2	3	4	5
3. content of registration packet	1	2	3	4	5
4. route map	1	2	3	4	5
5. registration event day	1	2	3	4	5
6. receiving a t-shirt event day	1	2	3	4	5
7. route	1	2	3	4	5
8. length of route	1	2	3	4	5
9. rest stops	1	2	3	4	5
10. rest stop food	1	2	3	4	5
11. route volunteers	1	2	3	4	5
12. lunch at finish	1	2	3	4	5

What part of the event did you enjoy the *most*? _____

_____

What part of the event did you enjoy the *least*? _____

_____

Additional comments:

(optional)

name_____

address_____

_____

telephone_____

■

count me in!
I would like to
join next year's
planning committee

participant evaluation

(Exhibit 12.1) This participant evaluation form allows people to voice their dissatisfaction with the event in a productive way, and you benefit by considering their suggestions or solving the problem for next year.

Evaluation by Statistics

The only quantifiable way to evaluate your event is by event statistics. While these stats cannot tell you how effective your logistics or public relations campaign were, they will give you hard numbers which will determine the financial success of your event. Exhibit 12.2 provides a sample analysis of participants and their pledges. Refer back to Chapter 4 for other techniques to capture the data.

Stats You'll Want *(and Need)* to Capture

Basic

- Number of pre-registered participants
- Number of walk-on participants
- Total number of participants
- Amount pledged by pre-registered participants
- Amount pledged by walk-on participants
- Total pledged
- Dollar amount turned in
- Total due
- Average pledge per participant
- Average pledge per pre-registered participant
- Average pledge per walk-on participant

Complex

- No-shows to pre-registered participant ratio
- Walk-on to pre-registered participant ratio
- Gross expense as a percentage of gross income
- Where participant heard about the event

All of the above stats can easily be read and evaluated by using any spreadsheet program, e.g., Lotus.

STATS
for entries as of: _____

PARTICIPANT PLEDGE ANALYSIS
by ROUTE

Route(s)	Total # walk participants	Total # paid participants	% paid participants	Day of walk	Current pledge	Non-participant donations	Total pledges paid	Total pledges & donations paid	% of pledges collected	Average pledge paid
Northern										
Route A	3,358	2,556	76.1%	378,125	399,109	6,916	397,781	404,697	105.3%	158.33
Route B	215	195	83.9%	30,020	27,591	235	24,528	24,863	82.3%	127.50
Route C										
Route D										
Route I										
Sub-total										
Central Area										
Route E	177	132	74.6%	22,269	23,407	101	16,533	16,634	74.2%	125.25
Sub-total										
Southern										
Route F	914	857	88.8%	84,087	84,087	1,326	83,673	84,999	99.5%	99.18
Sub-total										
GRAND TOTAL	4,664	3,740	323.4%	514,501	534,194	8,578	522,515	531,193	361.3%	510.26

(Exhibit 12.2) Here is a sample pledge analysis. Capturing statistics like these is important to determine whether your event was financially successful, and it can help you figure out any changes for your next event.

Thirteen

Pledge Collection

Collecting 110% of Your Pledges

Finally . . . pledge collection. An event can be the greatest ever, logistically, thousands can show up and have the time of their lives. Many large corporate teams can show up and pledge thousands. These are all wonderful things, *but if pledges are not collected, the event is not a success.* We are all part of money-driven organizations and we must get the most money at the least cost. It's that simple. If we plan ahead, pledge collection is simple. Often, however, we wait and try to "catch up" when it's too late.

Read the following strategies for pledge collection. Adopt them. Use them. Here's a basic, but foolproof, system for collecting 110% of your pledges. How can we collect 110%? It's easy, especially if your event has taken place before. Past participants not only return the highest pledges, but their pledge average is always significantly higher than other groups. Also, collect from people who never showed up. Don't forget any group. Ask volunteers to raise money. But most important, be prepared. Make sure your pledge collection direct mail pieces are pre-printed and ready to go according to the pledge collection timeline.

Pledge Collection Timeline

Day after event	Mail pledge cards back to participants
1 week after	Mail "we missed you" letter to all no-shows
3 weeks after	Friendly plea (letter) to all past participants who did not return
3 weeks after	Reminder postcard to all no-pays that pledges are due the next week (humorous)
5 weeks after	Mail humorous chaser postcards to all no-pays and apologize if their payment crossed in the mail
5 weeks after	Humorous chaser postcard to all people who paid, but paid less than what they had pledged (can have negative effect)
7 weeks *and* *ongoing*	Tele-collecting: Begin calling top pledgers first, then go down the line to people who pledged the least
8 weeks after	Mail chaser letter with pre-paid envelope; include another prize form and let them know the prize deadline will be extended for them
9 weeks after	*Serious* chaser letter with return envelope

Day-of Incentives for Turning in Pledges

There are a number of ways to encourage participants to turn in pledges on event day. Here are a few:

- The single most effective incentive is to hand out the event t-shirt on event day if participants turn in at least X amount

of their pledges. Usually this amount is the exact amount
to receive a t-shirt (usually $50 or more).

- Offer special day-of *extra* incentives for people who turn
  in $100 or more. These incentives can be anything from a
  sponsored hat to a button or water bottle.
- "Advertise" in all pre-walk newsletters that all walkers
  who turn in $100 or more will be automatically entered
  into a raffle for a trip or substantial electronic item (donated, of course!).

Collecting from No-Shows

Often, people who have not shown up have good reasons.
Once, I was so disappointed with the show-up rate, my committee
and I called every no-show. Most reasons were very believable —
usually they were sick or overslept. The most encouraging news
from these calls was that these no-shows had already collected
some or all of their pledges. Rather than have them return these
pledges to their owners, it's critical to have a pre-prepared letter
(and a finish kit), asking the no-show to walk in his or her
neighborhood.

Dealing with Deadbeats

Unfortunately, charity pledge-based events are not immune
to dead-beats (no-pays). While you may feel there are no alternatives, I challenge you to consider the following tactics:

- Revoke deadbeats' rights to participate again. Be sure to
  check new registrations against no-pay list.
- As a last resort, and after numerous letters, cards, and volunteers' calls, turn the call over to a professional telemarketing firm (not a collection firm). Be careful, however —
  do this only if you are certain your systems are up to date
  and you have kept stellar records.

Resources

The Orensof Groupe
Computer and internet consulting firm. Provides group internet services to nonprofits.
670 Aberdeen Lane, Buffalo Grove, IL 60089
Telephone (500) Orensof
Website: charityevents.com
Max Bar-Nahum, president

Ideas To Go, Inc.
Creative agency
One Main at Riverplace, Suite 504
Minneapolis, MN 55414
Telephone 612.331.1570
Fred S. Meyer, principal

Internal Revenue Service
Assistant Commissioner
Employee Plans & Tax Exempt Organizations
Attention: E:EO:P
Washington, D.C. 20224
Telephone 202.566.6356

IEG, Inc.
International Events Group
640 North LaSalle
Suite 600
Chicago, IL 60610-3777
Telephone 312.944.1727
IEG publishes the following:
  IEG Sponsorship Report
  IEG's Complete Guide to Sponsorship
  IEG Sponsorship Sourcebook
  IEG Legal Guide to Sponsorship
  IEG Sponsordex/IEG Sponsordisk
  IEG Event Marketing Conference
  IEG Sponsorship Workshop Series
  IEG Consulting

Nancy Roberts Linder
Nancy Roberts Linder Consulting
Marketing consultant and internet specialist
119 Bassford Avenue
LaGrange, IL 60525
Telephone 708.482.0760
Facsimile 708.482.0761
E-mail: nrl@nrlinder.com.

American Marketing Association
Marketing News
250 South Wacker Drive
Chicago, Illinois 60606
Telephone 312.648.0536

First Nonprofit Companies
First Nonprofit Insurance Company, a reciprocal First Nonprofit Trust, is owned by nonprofits, governed by nonprofits, and dedicated to the nonprofit community
111 North Canal Street, Suite 801
Chicago, Illinois 60606
Telephone 312.627.7724
Facsimile 312.930.0376

Risk Management and Information Systems, Inc.
Risk management consulting firm
105 West Adams
Chicago, Illinois 60603
Telephone 312.251.1065
Celeste Watts, president

The Touch of Treuhaft
Communications specialists
1918 West Eddy Street
Chicago, Illinois 60657
Telephone 312.477.7918
E-mail: 75150,1567@compuserve.com
Janet Treuhaft, principal

Bibliography

Applied Imagination, Alex F. Osborn, Charles Scribner's Sons, New York, 1953

Healthy, Wealthy and Wise, Weamanship, Inc., Salem (OR), 1995

Internet for Dummies, John Levine, IDG Books, Indianapolis, 1996

Let's Talk Quality, Philip B. Crosby, McGraw-Hill, Inc., New York, 1989

Navigating the Internet, John Levine, SAMS Publishing Group, Division of Prentice Hall Computer Publishing, Indianapolis, 1994

Successful Telemarketing, 1986, Stone, Bob and Wyman, John. NTC Business Books, Lincolnwood (IL), 1986

Weight Loss through Persistence, Daniel S. Kirschenbaum, Ph.D., New Harbinger Publications, Inc., Oakland, 1994

Index

T

U